COLONIAL

Georgia

Clifford Sheats Capps
Eugenia Burney

THOMAS NELSON INC.

Nashville / New York

All photographs courtesy of the Georgia Historical Society, with the exception of the following: pp: 10, 14, 15, National Park Service; p. 11, Georgia Department of Industry and Trade; pp. 32, 38, 39, 45, 129, 153, 154, 162, Georgia Historical Commission; p. 36, American Philosophical Society Library; pp. 49, 54, *The History of Our Country*, by Edward S. Ellis; p. 57, *The Darien News*; pp. 60, 64, 71, Fort Frederica National Monument; pp. 65, from the private collection of Burnett Van Storey; p. 80, Atlanta Archives; p. 122, Atlanta Historical Society. Permission is gratefully acknowledged.

917.58
CAP

Library of Congress Cataloging in Publication Data

Capps, Clifford Sheats
   Colonial Georgia.

   SUMMARY: Traces the history of Georgia from the first prehistoric settlers to the establishment of a state government following the Revolution.
   Bibliography: p.
   1. Georgia—History—Colonial period—Juvenile literature. [1. Georgia—History—Colonial period] I. Burney, Eugenia, joint author. II. Title.
F289.C33   917.58'03'2   73-181674
ISBN 0-8407-7112-6
ISBN 0-8407-7113-4 (NLB.)

Printed in the United States of America

TENNESSEE

NORTH CAROLINA

SOUTH CAROLINA

GEORGIA

STATE OF GEORGIA
CONSTITUTION
WISDOM · JUSTICE · MODERATION
1776

75

CARTERSVILLE
ETOWAH MOUNDS
ARCHAEOLOGICAL AREA

85

☆ATLANTA

20

85

EAGLE EFFIGY MOUND ▲

EATONTON

MEADOW GARDEN
AUGUSTA SIGNERS' MONUMENT
MACKAY HOUSE

Savannah River

N

▲ OCMULGEE
NATIONAL
MONUMENT

MACON

16

75

EBENEZER ●
SAVANNAH ● BETHESDA
BEAULIEU ▲
VERNONBURG
WORMSLOE PLANTATION
MIDWAY ●
MIDWAY MUSEUM ▲
FORT MORRIS ▲
DARIEN
FORT KING GEORGE ▲

ALABAMA

ATLANTIC
OCEAN

17

● Cities and Towns

▲ Historical Sites

FLORIDA

ST. SIMONS ISLAND

FORT FREDERICA
NATIONAL MONUMENT

BATTLE OF BLOODY MARSH
MONUMENT

Contents

CHAPTER ONE

Prehistoric Settlers

More than ten thousand years ago, long before men could write, the first settlers came to Georgia. Although we cannot learn of them from written records, they left their history in the things they made and the places in which they lived.

Archaeologists have learned that the first people came from Siberia to Alaska across the Bering Strait and then wandered all over North and South America. We call these people Indians, as Christopher Columbus mistakenly named them in 1492.

Although it may seem that we have little in common with these early Georgia settlers, they had the same needs that we have: food, shelter, clothes, and protection to ensure survival. Adults taught children skills needed to provide these necessities, and only by hard work and ingenuity did they manage to survive.

The Wandering Hunters

These first Americans used only a spear to kill the mammoth and bison they needed for food and materials. The spear was made by tying a

Tomochichi was more than ninety years old when he and Toonahowi, his nephew and adopted son, went to England with Oglethorpe and visited King George II. This portrait was painted during their stay in London.

sharp stone point on to a shaft of wood with a thong of skin or a piece of vine. It was thrown from a throwing stick called an *atlatl*, to give it more force. For variety in their diet, the Indians caught fish by using bone hooks on a line or woven nets. They used blowguns with poisoned darts to kill birds, turkeys, rabbits, and squirrels.

The women roasted the meat over an open fire or smoked it for future use on a rack made of green willow wood. They had no pottery vessels, but sometimes they stone-boiled the meat. They would dig a pit in the ground and line it with a skin to hold water and keep the dirt from the food. After filling the skin with water, they heated rocks and rolled them into the pit until the water was boiling. Pieces of meat with herbs for seasoning were put into the boiling water to cook. As the rocks in the pit cooled, they were removed and other hot rocks were put in. This was a slow and tedious method of cooking and was used less often than roasting.

These earliest Indians were called the Wandering Hunters. They moved from place to place, wherever game was to be found. Since large numbers of people could not move easily, each hunting band was made up of a few families.

The Shellfish Eaters

About six thousand years ago the Georgia Indians adopted a new eating habit which changed the pattern of their lives. Instead of depending on game for food, with a few fish for variety, they began to eat large quantities of shellfish: mussels, clams, and oysters. Not only were there shellfish near the ocean, but they found an abundant supply of fresh-water shellfish in the rivers. With this diet they no longer needed to move when game animals became scarce.

This change in eating habits altered the lives of the Georgia Indians in other ways. Larger groups lived at one place, and because food was easier to find, they had more time for dancing and playing games. One of the favorite games of both children and adults was a ball game. A tall

At the time white men first saw them, American Indians, played many ball games as well as other sports. This picture shows several different kinds of athletic activities going on at one time.

pole was erected in the middle of the village and a ball made of a wooden core wrapped with skin was hung from the top of the pole on a tough vine or thong. The contestants batted the ball back and forth with wooden paddles, each trying to make the ball wind around the pole in a different direction. The one who succeeded first won. The game of tetherball is a modern adaptation of this Indian game.

The Shellfish Eaters left their history in a much more concrete form than the Wandering Hunters. As they opened mollusks for food, they threw the shells to the ground around them. Over a period of years, the pile of shells built up until the Indians were living on top of shell mounds twenty to thirty feet high. Although the bones of fish, bear, rabbit, deer, turkey, and other game are mixed with the shells, the bulky shells are what created the mounds.

These Indians made vessels of soapstone or sandstone in which they stone-boiled food, and they made baskets and mats of woven reeds and grasses. Not until about 1500 B.C. did they learn to make pottery. This brought about another change in their lives. They could use pots over the fire for cooking. Therefore, stew became the mainstay of the menu, and since game, fish, and vegetables could all be put into the same pot, their diets became more nutritious and appetizing.

The Early Farmers

As the Indians settled down into villages, they began the cultivating of wild vegetables. They selected a place where no trees grew, dug some holes with their hands, and put seeds into them. They did not try to keep the weeds from growing but gathered whatever pumpkins, beans, and sunflowers ripened. The bow and arrow was invented at this time, and axes were fashioned from stone.

The pipes of the Early Farmers were straight tubes made of soapstone or steatite. Tobacco was packed into the end and lighted.

The famous Eagle Effigy Mound is located between Madison and Eatonton, Georgia. Made of white quartz boulders, it is 102 feet long and 120 feet wide.

They also grew tobacco. Dried tobacco leaves were smoked in a pipe, although these pipes were not the kind which we are accustomed to seeing today. The earliest form of pipe of the Georgia Indians was a straight tube made of soapstone or steatite, a compact form of talc. Both of these minerals are soft and easy to hollow out, and the tobacco was packed into the tube and lighted at the end. At first the pipes were used only by the shamans, medicine men who smoked them as part of their magic. Later the chiefs, who were called micos, and lesser chiefs smoked pipes as part of their council ceremony.

The Early Farmers built mounds of rock, called effigy mounds, representing animals or birds. Rocks or boulders were piled side by side about two feet high to make a solid form of the bird or animal representation desired. The rocks were so closely packed that no plants could grow between them, and thus they have been preserved for us to see.

When Jacob Le Moyne, a French artist, came to America with René de Laudonnière, he drew many pictures of the Guale Indians and their way of life. These drawings show the preparation of food. *Top:* Both baskets and pottery were used as containers. *Bottom:* To keep it from spoiling, meat was smoked on racks of green willow wood. The Spanish also cooked meat in this fashion. They called the frame a *barbacoa*, from which our word "barbecue" is derived.

Near Eatonton, Georgia, is the Eagle Effigy Mound. It is made of white quartz boulders in the shape of a spread eagle, 102 feet long and 120 feet wide.

The Master Farmers

About one hundred years before Leif Ericson came to America (about A.D. 900), a new group of migrating Indians moved into Georgia from the Mississippi Valley. The Early Farmers, who had lived along the Ocmulgee River for the preceding thousand years, resisted. But the Master Farmers had a much more sophisticated civilization and easily drove the Early Farmers to other parts of Georgia. They established a small village about five miles south of the present city of Macon and a larger village at what is now the Ocmulgee National Monument.

These farmers cultivated not only beans, pumpkins, sunflowers, and tobacco, as had the Early Farmers, but they added to their fields the vegetable which was to be named the staff of life of the New World: corn. Unlike the soft vegetables which had to be eaten before they spoiled, corn could be dried like peas and kept over the winter. Since corn could be grown in abundance, it was possible for many families to live together during the winter, sharing the dried corn instead of having to find enough roots and bark, or kill enough game to keep themselves alive. These larger groups had manpower and leisure with which to build religious and ceremonial structures.

The Master Farmers moved tons of earth to build mounds up to fifty feet high. These mounds are found not only in Georgia but extend from the northern part of Vermont to the Gulf of Mexico and the Rocky Mountains.

In the winter, the mico at Ocmulgee led his counselors and forty-seven warriors through a long, low tunnel into a circular room with a floor of hard-packed clay. Around the wall was a bench with forty-seven seats modeled in the clay, on which the warriors sat. The mico and his counselors mounted an earth platform which was built in the

13

This diorama at the Ocmulgee National Monument at Macon, Georgia, shows the inside of the earth lodge of the Master Farmers about A.D. 1100. The original lodge has been restored and is open to the public.

form of a spread eagle and extended from the back wall almost to the sunken fire pit in the center of the lodge, opposite the entrance.

The roof of this room consisted of a structure of woven reeds and saplings, over which a thick mound of earth was heaped, making the inside warm enough to be comfortable in the coldest weather. This earth lodge has been completely reconstructed on the basis of archaeological excavations, and the visitor may go inside it.

The potters of this period had a sense of humor. The decorations they attached to the edges of jars and bowls, often in the form of heads of wild animals such as foxes, owls, or ducks, had big staring eyes that peered down into the bowl. Pipes had changed from the simple tube to the shape we know today with a stem and bowl. They were molded from clay, and the stems were short—only one or two inches. The bowls were large and decorated like the pots with many shapes, such as the heads of birds and animals and even human heads with oversized, goggling eyes.

Ocmulgee was the center of Indian culture in Georgia at the time of the Master Farmers, who developed a form of civilization as advanced in many respects as any to be found north of Mexico. We do not know what happened to the Master Farmers. They lived less than two hundred years at Ocmulgee, after which the site was deserted for more than 250 years.

Uchees, Creeks, and Cherokees

The Uchee Indians, a small band who lived along the Oconee and the headwaters of the Ogeechee and Chattahoochee rivers, were all that remained of a once powerful tribe. They claimed to be more ancient

The pipes of the Master Farmers were shaped with stems and bowls. They were decorated with the heads of birds, mammals, or humans with big, goggling eyes.

Two Le Moyne drawings. *Top:* The houses of the Indians of Guale were built with clay walls and thatched roofs. Boats were made by hollowing out large logs, often cypress. *Bottom:* When hunting alligators, the Indians would force a long pole into the animal's mouth, making it impossible for it to bite. Then they turned the beast over on its back, so they could kill it through the soft belly instead of trying to pierce the thick hide.

than the surrounding people, and they bordered the Cherokees in the northwestern part of Georgia.

The Creeks were the most powerful tribe. They occupied the Atlantic Coast from the mouth of the Cape Fear River to the end of the Florida peninsula. They called themselves Este Muskokee and claimed to have come out of the earth. Their legends said that they had migrated from the far northwest until they reached Florida, then retreated and took possession of the region extending east to the Ocmulgee River and west to the Coosa and Tallapoosa rivers. This country had many creeks and rivulets and was called by the early explorers the Creek Country. So the Indians came to be known as Creek Indians.

The Cherokees called themselves Tsaraghee. They occupied the upper valley of the Tennessee River, the mountains and valleys of the Allegheny Range, and the headwaters of the Savannah River. Their legends told how they, too, had migrated from the west but much earlier than the Creeks. They insisted that they had driven out a moon-eyed people who were unable to see by day.

By the time Christopher Columbus discovered Hispaniola and Cuba in 1492, Georgia had been populated for ten thousand years from the islands of the seacoast to the northwestern mountains. It was not until almost one hundred years later, however, that the Indians were to meet the white man with his greed for gold.

CHAPTER TWO

The Spanish Settle Guale

For two hundred years before Christopher Columbus set sail across the Atlantic Ocean to seek Asia, men had been excited by a description written by Marco Polo, a Venetian, of the golden treasures of the East after his stay in China and India from 1275 to 1292. When Columbus discovered Hispaniola, thinking it to be Asia, he expected to find as much gold as Marco Polo had seen. Although he found only little pieces of gold worn in the noses of the natives, it was enough to start the rumor.

Cities of Gold

After Columbus died, his son Diego, viceroy of the West Indies, sent Diego Velázquez to conquer Cuba. Velázquez sent Hernando Cortés to conquer Mexico, which had been discovered only recently. Cortés landed at Tabasco, where he subdued the natives and learned of Montezuma, the emperor, who lived in a city of gold treasures. Cortés arrested Montezuma and demanded all of his gold.

After Cortés described to the king of Spain this country of five million people who had golden ornaments and images so heavy that two men were needed to carry them, word spread all over Europe. Men deserted their work and farms, and anyone who could buy passage to Santo Domingo thought himself already rich. The first gold rush of the New World had begun.

Three Countries Claim America

John Cabot, an Italian navigator who had moved to Bristol, England, persuaded Henry VII to give him a discover's license. As captain of the small ship *Matthew* he sailed west and sighted what is now Canada on June 24, 1497. This voyage gave England the basis for her claim to America.

Juan Ponce de León, a Spanish nobleman, heard of a spring of water which restored youth to old men who drank of it. He obtained a license from the king of Spain to discover the fountain of youth. On Easter Sunday, 1513, he sighted the coast of what is now Florida and named it *Pascua Florida* which means Feast of Flowers. He claimed the whole country for Spain.

By 1521 the merchant ships of Spain were filled with gold from South America. Another Italian, Giovanni da Verrazano, who worked as a navigator for Francis I, king of France, captured a Spanish ship loaded with treasure valued at $1,500,000. The king was pleased with

Hernando de Soto, who led an expedition through Georgia and almost halfway across the continent in search of gold which he never found.

Verrazano's piracy and sent him across the Atlantic in the *Dauphine* to look for a passage to China in the area north of the region Spain claimed. In March, 1524, Verrazano reached the American coast at what is now North Carolina. He went as far north as Nova Scotia and claimed the land for France.

Now three European kingdoms claimed North America, and 150 years would pass with much bloodshed before these three would lose their possessions and a new independent nation would be born.

A Rich Man Wants to Get Richer

If Mexico was so rich, Florida must be filled with gold also. This was the reasoning of Don Hernando de Soto, who was born in Spain about 1496. He had gone with an expedition to explore the coast of Central America and had also been a leader in the capture of Cuzco, Peru, the capital of the Incas.

De Soto returned to Spain when he was about thirty-five years old. He was then so wealthy that King Charles V borrowed money from him, but De Soto longed to be richer. He believed that Florida had more gold than both Mexico and Peru, so he offered to conquer it at his own expense. The king gave him permission and made him governor of Cuba.

Hundreds of young men asked to go with him. The wealthier ones wore suits of armor and were followed by servants. With these men, his young wife, and other noble ladies, De Soto sailed from Spain early in April, 1538, with seven large and three small ships, the *San Christoval* being his flagship. There was much gaiety, and the ladies and gentlemen spent most of their time on board feasting and enjoying music and dancing as they made their way across the Atlantic Ocean.

Near the end of May the fleet reached Cuba, and a year later De Soto left with nine ships bearing six hundred soldiers, twelve priests, four friars, two secretaries, servants, cattle, horses, mules, and bloodhounds. He also took with him thirteen sows and several boars, the first hogs to

De Soto brought about two hundred horses with him in his search for gold. By the end of the expedition, only forty were left, and they were lame, having gone for a year without shoes.

be seen on the American continent. The fleet sailed north from Havana and landed near what is now Tampa, Florida.

A detailed description of the journey was written by a Portuguese secretary, who did not leave his name but signed his daily report simply "A Gentleman of Elvas." Much of the information about De Soto's journey comes from his writing.

The Indians fled as De Soto disembarked. He took over their deserted town, destroying the buildings, and sent men to capture Indians for questioning. The horsemen found several natives, and one man cried out to them in Spanish. He was naked, sunburned, and tattooed, and looked like the Indians, but his name was Juan Ortiz, and he had been a member of a Spanish expedition nine years before. He had lived with the Indians ever since and spoke their language like a native. De Soto was delighted to find Ortiz and took him along as interpreter. As the Spaniards marched across what is now Florida, the Gentleman of Elvas wrote in his journal that two captains were sent to capture Indians. A hundred men and women were taken. The Spaniards put iron collars around their necks and fastened them together with chains. They were forced to carry the luggage and grind corn like slaves.

In October the Spaniards reached Apalachee, near where Tallahassee, Florida, is today. They set up winter quarters and remained there until March 3, 1540. Most of the Indians they had enslaved died during the winter from lack of food and from working naked in chains. Now the soldiers were forced to carry the corn in addition to their arms and other gear. De Soto would not allow a single hog to be killed, even though the original thirteen sows had multiplied to three hundred.

The army spent the night of March 4 on the Ochlockonee River. The next morning they started the four-month march across what is now Georgia.

The Spanish infantry dressed in colorful uniforms with slashed doublet and hose. Even in the heat of Georgia summers they marched through the forests in full dress.

The Dog Eaters

Without meat and salt, many men died from malnutrition. The soldiers craved meat so badly that, when they arrived at a town and found twenty or thirty dogs, they killed and cooked them to eat.

The Indians shot deer, turkeys, rabbit, and other wild game, but the Spaniards on the march did not have time to hunt. Nor did they dare to straggle off for fear of being killed by the Indians. Still De Soto would not allow any hogs to be killed for food. How they were tended and driven is not known. They ate the acorns from the forest floor and were perhaps fed corn when enough was available.

Marching, resting, and fighting, the expedition passed through what is now Calhoun and Dougherty counties. For ten days more the hungry men and lean horses marched toward Ocute in present-day Laurens County. As the tired Spaniards came near the town, two thousand Indians met them, bringing loaves of corn bread, partridges, turkeys, and dogs. Perhaps they had heard of the Spaniards' eating dogs and thought they liked them, or, since the Indians themselves ate dogs from time to time, usually in a ceremonial feast, they may have wanted to honor the Spaniards. De Soto and his men rested for two days, and when they left, the chief gave the Spaniards four hundred bearers.

They followed the Ocmulgee River past what is now Hawkinsville. But still they did not find any gold. Although some of the men begged De Soto to turn back, he urged them on. They forded the Ogeechee River near where Louisville now stands, then Briar Creek.

Four captured Indians refused to give any information, and De Soto ordered one of them to be burned alive. The others finally said that two days' journey would bring them to the province called Cutifachiqui (the Creek word for Dogwood Town), which was supposed to be very wealthy. With this good news, De Soto decided that some of the hogs could be killed. Each man was allotted a half pound of pork per day, and this, with boiled wild spinach, was now their diet.

The Queen of Dogwood Town

De Soto was now in a province where a woman reigned. When the Spaniards arrived on the banks of the Rio Dulce (Savannah River), south of present-day Augusta, they saw four canoes approaching. In the first was an Indian princess who welcomed De Soto in the name of her sister, the queen.

The princess was followed by the queen herself, seated on cushions in a canoe with an awning over it. She welcomed De Soto and took a string of large pearls from around her neck and placed it over De Soto's head. De Soto gave the queen a ring of gold set with a ruby as a token of peace and friendship.

When the queen saw how much the Spaniards valued the pearls, she told De Soto that there were many more buried in the tombs of dead Indians. She gave him permission to go to an uninhabited town nearby, dig up the graves, and take all he could find. The men dug wildly and found over 350 pounds of pearls.

The queen had not foreseen that they would completely desecrate the sacred tombs, but the Spaniards considered the Indians savages, and nothing of their culture was sacred to them. Looting and raping followed the treasure hunt, and even the Gentleman of Elvas was shocked at the behavior of the Spaniards.

Many of the men begged De Soto to settle in Cutifachiqui, but the conquistador had not found the gold he wanted so badly. After a few days' rest, De Soto demanded bearers from the queen, but she refused because of the treatment of her people by the Spaniards. De Soto took the queen with him as a hostage to force her people to give him supplies. She was made to travel on foot with some of her women attendants, one of whom carried a box filled with the most valuable pearls.

De Soto planned to take the pearls from the queen after he had finished using her, but the queen had other plans. One day she asked permission to go into the woods for a few minutes to take care of a private matter. Her women went with her, including the one with the pearls. They failed to return, and even the bloodhounds could not track them through the swamps. They were never seen again by the Spaniards, but they returned safely to Cutifachiqui.

End of the Search

On and on marched the Spaniards. De Soto led them north to the border of Georgia and on into Tennessee. He came back south through what is now Rome, Georgia, and went on into present-day Alabama and Mississippi. Finally they reached the banks of a river which we know now as the Mississippi. Boats were built to cross it, and in 1541 the Spaniards entered Arkansas.

After a hard winter, De Soto decided to give up his search for gold and to turn back toward the sea. He was sick with fever and gave his command to one of his captains. On May 21, 1542, he died.

The captains did not want the Indians to know that their leader was

The Queen of Dogwood Town.   25 dead, so in the middle of the night they placed his body in a canoe weighted with sand and towed it to the middle of the Mississippi River, where it was sunk.

De Soto's property was sold at auction, including the seven hundred hogs he owned. After the auction, the men ate all the pork they wanted.

Learning from the white men, the Indians took to raising hogs themselves. Some pigs escaped and ran wild. It is said that the vicious wild hogs in the Okefenokee Swamp, known there as "Piney Woods Rooters," are descended from De Soto's droves.

Spanish and French Colonies Fail

King Philip II of Spain was so enraged by French and English attacks on Spanish ships that were bringing gold from Mexico that he decided to make settlements along the southern coast of the North American mainland to protect Spanish interests. In 1559 he sent Tristán de Luna to what is now Georgia, but, like De Soto, De Luna failed, and he left the area in April, 1561.

At this time the Catholic Church in France was doing its best to wipe out the Protestants called Huguenots. In 1562 one of the Huguenot leaders, Gaspard de Coligny, arranged for a group to go to America, and he sent Jean Ribaut and a few gentlemen of fortune to find a suitable place for a colony. They built a fort near Port Royal in what is today South Carolina. Ribaut left thirty men to hold it until he could return to France and bring colonists, but the men tired of waiting and abandoned the fort before he returned.

St. Augustine Founded

Two years later, in 1564, another expedition, under René de Laudonnière, landed at the mouth of the St. Johns River and built a fort which was named Caroline. Along with Laudonnière was an artist named Jacob Le Moyne, who drew many interesting pictures of the Indians and animals of the New World.

When Jean Ribaut brought the first French settlers to America, he built a stone pillar on which he put the French coat of arms, claiming the country for France. Even though the colony was abandoned, the Indians continued to bring gifts and lay them at the foot of the pillar in reverence.

Because the Indians were not friendly, Laudonnière decided to leave Fort Caroline, but pirates had taken one of the ships and they had to build another before they could return to France. Laudonnière and the colonists were ready to abandon the country when Jean Ribaut sailed into the harbor with three hundred Huguenot colonists.

A week later a Spanish fleet attacked the French ships. Admiral Pedro Menéndez had been sent by Philip II to drive the French out of Florida. Against the advice of Laudonnière, Jean Ribaut resisted the Spaniards, but his ships were wrecked by a storm, and Ribaut and about seven hundred of his men swam ashore. They started walking toward Fort Caroline.

Having seen the French fleet destroyed, Menéndez landed his forces south of Fort Caroline and claimed the country for Spain. Thus was founded the city of St. Augustine, oldest city in what is today the United States. It was to remain the capital of the Spanish colonies in Florida, which included Georgia, for 150 years. Menéndez ordered a fort to be built and immediately left with a company of soldiers to attack the heretics at Fort Caroline.

Massacre of the Huguenots

The Spaniards captured the fort easily and asked if the French were Catholics or Protestants. The Huguenots replied staunchly that they were Protestants. They were murdered on the spot, and the Spaniards hung many of the bodies upon trees, marked with an inscription saying that they had been slain not as Frenchmen but as Lutherans. (They were actually Calvinists, but the Spanish did not acknowledge such niceties.) Laudonnière and Le Moyne managed to escape and return to France.

As Menéndez marched back toward his new fort at St. Augustine, he met Jean Ribaut and his forces. He asked them the same question he had asked the Huguenots at Fort Caroline. A few men said that they were Catholics, but the remainder admitted they were Protestants. The Spanish commander ordered that they be put to death.

Three years later, a French sea captain put in at Fort Caroline, seized the garrison the Spanish had left behind, and killed them. He, too, put up an inscription. It said that the Spaniards had been slain not as Spaniards but as murderers.

The Land of Guale

North of the St. Johns River lay the Indian land of Guale. If the English had first made a map of this area, they would have spelled it "Walley," because that is how they would have pronounced it. The Spanish pronounced it the same way, but they spelled it Guale.

In 1566 Menéndez visited the land of Guale. He sailed north up the coast to talk with the Indians about building forts on their islands. He also tried to tell the Indians about the Catholic religion, but they were not interested.

Menéndez was convinced that the Indians must be taught Catholicism, but in a letter to a Jesuit friend in Spain he said that it was impossible to teach the Holy Gospel with soldiers. He must have priests as missionaries.

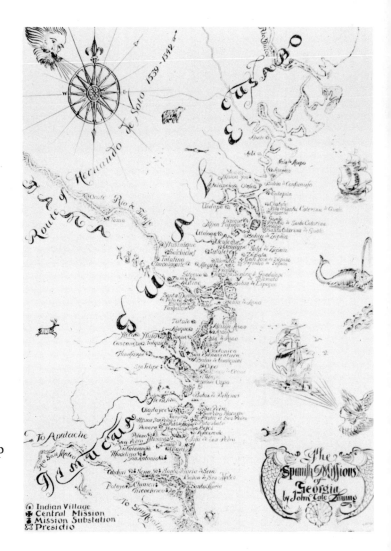

The land of Guale as shown on Spanish maps. It extended from the River Dulce (Savannah River) to the southern tip of Santa Catalina Island.

The Jesuit missionaries were among the first Europeans to come to the land of Guale, but the Indians were more interested in the gifts the Spaniards gave them than in the priests' promises of salvation.

The Jesuits Fail

A year and eight months after Menéndez first landed in Florida, he set sail for Spain for a visit with his wife and the king. He was rewarded by the king for having slaughtered the heretics, and his portrait was painted by the famous artist Titian.

While he was in Spain, Menéndez worked hard to secure missionaries for Guale. When he sailed for St. Augustine on March 13, 1568, ten Jesuits went with him.

Father Sedeno and Brother Baez were sent to Guale. Brother Baez learned the Gualean language, then wrote an Indian grammar and translated a catechism. Before the end of the year, however, he died of malarial fever, and Father Sedeno returned to St. Augustine.

In two years the missionaries had baptized only seven persons. In

1572 all of the Jesuit missionaries were ordered to Mexico City. Governor Menéndez died in 1574, and Spain seemed to have deserted the eastern mainland of North America.

The Franciscans Arrive

Late in 1577, Father Alonso de Reynoso arrived in St. Augustine with several Franciscan priests. For the next eight years he worked among the Indians in Guale, and in 1586 he returned to Spain to ask the king for more missionaries.

Meanwhile, England had been watching Spain's colonization of Florida and Guale, and in 1586 Queen Elizabeth sent Sir Francis Drake to America to wipe out St. Augustine. Drake arrived with an English fleet and completely destroyed the town and fort.

An artist's concept of a mission in Guale. The missionaries often erected a cross of whole trees to symbolize Christianity.

The new governor, Pedro Menéndez Marqués, called the soldiers from all the presidios in Guale, and in July of 1586 he began the construction of a stone castle-fortress at St. Augustine.

The commissar of the Indies sent twelve friars under Father Juan de Silva to Guale to build missions on San Pedro (Cumberland), Ospo (Jekyll), and Asao (St. Simons) islands. The priests took over the Indian festivals, marriages, births, and funerals, combining the Mass with dances and festivities. Helped by the background the Jesuits had laid years before, the Franciscans were now able to convert hundreds of Indians to Catholicism.

The Juanillo Revolt

As the priests assumed more power, many of the younger Indians began to protest. When the old mico of Guale died, his son Juanillo expected to become head mico, but Juanillo was a militant young Indian who had defied the missionaries many times. Therefore, Father Corpa appointed as head mico of Guale Don Francisco, a much older man who had always been submissive to the priests.

The militants put on their war paint, took their bows and arrows, and went to Tolomato during the night and hid in the church where they knew Father Corpa came every morning to say Mass. On the morning of September 13, 1597, as the unsuspecting priest opened the door of his church, they killed him with a club.

These pottery shards, found at Fort King George, are part of a Spanish olive jar. It is believed that this vessel was used at the Spanish mission between 1650 and 1686.

But Juanillo did not intend to stop with the murder of a single priest. From Tolomato the warriors advanced on Tupique. They allowed Father Rodriguez to sing a last Mass, and when he had finished, they killed him. The Indians threw his body into a field to be eaten by wild beasts and carrion birds, after which they went to Santa Catalina Island, where they made quick work of killing the two missionaries there.

Father Velascola, prie' on Asao Island, was in St. Augustine. The Indians hid in a clump f reeds near the water, and when Velascola rowed his boat to the landing, several of the Indians caught him by the shoulders, and others chopped his body into small pieces with their tomahawks. When they attacked Father Francisco Davila on Ospo Island, one of the micos interceded, and Davila was carried as a slave to an interior village, from which he was later rescued.

Although San Pedro Island was so near St. Augustine, success gave the Indians courage to attack it. On October 4, 1597, they manned forty canoes with warriors, but a Spanish brigantine anchored nearby, which they thought was filled with Spaniards, made them hesitate to attack.

The governor sent groups of soldiers to destroy the Indian villages, public buildings, and granaries. Juanillo and his followers fled to the interior of Guale and entrenched themselves in a stockaded town called Yfusinique. Don Francisco gathered a force of Indians and attacked the town. When the battle was over, they found Juanillo's body, cut off his scalp, and took it to St. Augustine to show to the Spaniards.

The Bishop Visits Guale

The Franciscans had long wanted a bishop to visit Guale to confirm some of the several thousands of natives they had converted. In 1605 Bishop Fray Juan de las Cabezas Altamirano of Havana received orders from the king of Spain to visit the mainland. He reached St. Augustine in the middle of March, 1606, the first bishop ever to visit the North American mainland. Everywhere the Indians flocked to see him, and more than fifteen hundred were confirmed.

In 1612 twenty-three Franciscan friars arrived, followed the next year by eight more. Twelve others arrived in 1615. New missions were built as far as the Chattahoochee region on the southern and western boundaries of modern Georgia.

For the next fifty-five years the missions continued to succeed. Although there were occasional Indian uprisings, they were quickly put down by the Spanish soldiers in the presidios.

An Englishman Arrives

Although Spain was now stronger than ever in Florida and Guale, England had been busy along the northern coast of the North American mainland. In 1607 the first permanent English colony had been founded at Jamestown, Virginia. The Dutch had set up a trading post on Manhattan Island in 1612, and in 1620 the Pilgrims landed at Plymouth, Massachusetts.

By 1630 the English colonial population in North America was es-

When Mark Catesby, an Englishman, visited what later became Georgia, he made this sketch of a woods bison. He described the buffalo as being so large that its skin was too heavy for the strongest man to lift from the ground. Not as plentiful as in the West, the bison was soon exterminated in Georgia.

timated at 5,700. In the next thirty-three years, Maryland, Rhode Island, Delaware, Connecticut, and New Jersey were established as English colonies, and the colonial population had jumped to 84,800. The Spaniards numbered fewer than 2,000 soldiers and priests. They did not bring farmers as settlers but depended on the Indians for labor.

About 1638, an Indian boy was born in Guale who would be important nearly one hundred years later—not to the Spaniards but to the English. He was named Tomochichi.

In 1663 Captain Robert Sandford, an Englishman, sailed from Barbados to survey the coast of Carolina, north of Guale, for a prospective colony. With him was a surgeon, Dr. Henry Woodward. Dr. Woodward wanted to stay with the Indians to study them. The mico made a place for Dr. Woodward beside him on his throne and told the people that Woodward would take the place of his sister's son, whom he would send with Sandford to be educated in England. Woodward lived with the Indians, learned their language, and studied their methods of raising crops.

The Spaniards heard that an Englishman was living in what they claimed to be their country. The governor sent an expedition to capture him, and Dr. Woodward was taken to St. Augustine. A few months later the English buccaneer Robert Searle surprised and captured the town of St. Augustine and released all the prisoners. He took Dr. Woodward to the Leeward Islands.

In 1670, when the English established a colony at Charles Town (now Charleston), South Carolina, Dr. Woodward returned with the first settlers. Since he had lived with the Indians before, he began going into the back country to renew friendships with them. It was not long before he crossed the Rio Dulce and began to make friends with the Indians of Guale.

At the same time, the French were making settlements and building forts along the Mississippi River to the west. The Spanish were being squeezed on both sides.

The animals native to Georgia, from a book on the natural history of the region by John Brickell, published in Dublin in 1737.

Withdrawal of the Missions

In 1682, Dr. Woodward with a half-dozen traders arrived at Coweta on the Chattahoochee River. General Matheos de Chuba took 250 Indians and a force of Spaniards from Apalachee and started out to capture this upstart Englishman as an example to the Indians who dealt with him.

De Chuba soon learned that he was playing a game of hide-and-seek. When he approached Coweta, the English and their Indian allies fled into the woods. Woodward sent a note to De Chuba saying that his company was not large enough to greet the Spaniard as he would like, but that he hoped to meet him at a later date. De Chuba destroyed a half-finished fort, but before he had returned to his headquarters, Woodward was going about his business, laughing at the Spaniard.

The Spaniards used the only retaliatory device they knew. They punished the Indians who traded with the English. Once a year for the next five years they sent punitive expeditions among the Indians of Guale, but the English maintained their friendship with the Indians by

36

selling them goods at a reasonable price and buying their furs. The Spaniards were afraid to arm the Indians, but the English sold them guns.

The Yemassee Indians drew closer to the English, and after several raids by them under English leadership, the missions at Asao, Tolomato, Santa Catalina, and Zapala were abandoned.

The Carolina governor, Joseph Blake, now brazenly claimed Apalachicola, the northwestern part of Guale, as part of Carolina, and later Governor John Archdale went so far as to forbid the Spaniards to come into the Apalachicola country which they had held for so many years.

Governor Moore's Raids

The English at Charles Town were as afraid of a Spanish attack as the Spaniards at St. Augustine were of an English attack. In 1702 Governor James Moore of South Carolina decided that the destruction of St. Augustine was the only way to ensure English domination of the coast.

He assembled a force of a thousand, half Englishmen and half Indian, and sailed down the coast of Guale to the bar at St. Augustine. Meanwhile, he sent Colonel Robert Daniel overland with one hundred white and Indian warriors. The Spaniards retreated before Colonel Daniel, and Governor Moore took the city of St. Augustine. For three months they laid siege to the stone castle-fort, but eventually the arrival of a Spanish man-of-war forced them to abandon the project. This raid pushed the Spanish frontier back to the St. Johns River.

The following year Governor Moore commanded an expedition against the province of Apalachee, the Spanish bulwark between Carolina and the French on the Gulf of Mexico, where the Georgia-Florida boundary is today. He passed through Ocmulgee and defeated Friar Angel de Miranda.

The land of Guale was now deserted by both the Spaniards and Indians. Thirty years passed before the English decided to colonize this no-man's-land.

CHAPTER THREE

Georgia—The Thirteenth Colony

After the Spaniards withdrew from Guale, the English at Charles Town decided to lay claim to the coast as far south as the Altamaha River, where Darien, Georgia, is now located, since it was the southern boundary of their grant. They were afraid the French would expand from the Mississippi River and make colonies along the Altamaha to link their holdings with the Atlantic Ocean.

"Plan of King George's Fort at Altamaha, South Carolina," a drawing by Colonel John Barnwell of South Carolina. The Carolinians claimed all the land to the Altamaha River because it had been in their original grant.

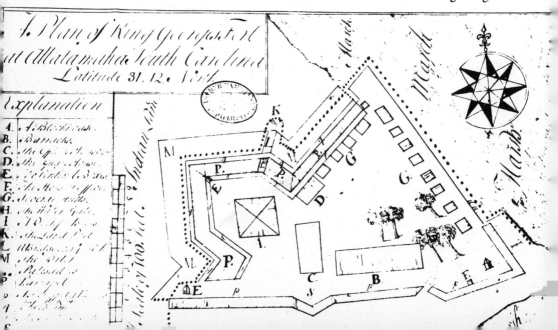

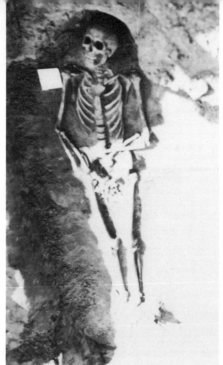

Skeletons of soldiers who died at Fort King George. Two lookouts were kept at the fort by the Carolinians until 1733, when Oglethorpe made his colony at Savannah.

Carolinians Move into Guale

In 1720 Colonel John Barnwell of Carolina went to England to appear before the Board of Trade and get permission to build a fort on the north bank of the Altamaha River on what was known as the Lower Bluff. The Board of Trade approved, and the following summer Colonel Barnwell and a group of Carolinians began the construction of Fort King George.

The fort was composed of a gabled blockhouse built of cypress planks sawed at the site. It was three stories high and armed with cannon. For six years Fort King George was garrisoned by the English, and when the troops were moved to Port Royal to help protect the plantations there, two lookouts were kept at the fort until 1733.

Trade with the Indians

After Henry Woodward made friends with the Indians in Guale, the South Carolina traders kept up a brisk business with them. One of the most successful was George Galphin, who had been born in Ireland and came to South Carolina when he was a young man. He settled at Silver Bluff, a trading post on the Carolina side of the Savannah River, where the famous Indian town of Cutifachiqui was located. Galphin soon had a thriving trade with the Indians and established another post, which he named Galphinton, on the Ogeechee River about fifty miles south-west of Augusta.

Another trading post was located at Yamacraw Bluff on the south side of the Savannah River. It was run by a Carolinian named John Musgrove and his half-Indian wife, Mary. A small band of Yamacraw Indians, of which Tomochichi was chief, lived in a village nearby.

South Carolinians were feeling more and more possessive of the southern territory since its desertion by the Spanish when events in England brought about a great change in the land of Guale.

England's Problem of Debt

Unemployment was a big problem in England in the early seventeen hundreds. Thousands of men were out of work, and when a man could not pay his bills, he was put into prison.

More than four thousand persons a year were put in debtors' prison in London alone. Hundreds of these men were the victims of speculations to which the government had given charters. Many others were made penniless by the collapse of the South Sea Company. These were men of aristocratic and once wealthy families, but when they lost their money or through negligence did not pay their bills, the English debtor laws demanded that they be put into prison. Soon the prisons were overflowing, and Parliament decided that something must be done.

James Edward Oglethorpe was a member of Parliament. He had a friend named Robert Castell, a well-known architect, who had pro-

40

James Edward Oglethorpe was both a philanthropist and a military man. This combination of characteristics enabled him to establish the colony of Georgia and build defenses that protected her from her enemies, the Spanish.

duced a beautiful book called *The Villas of the Ancients Illustrated*, with many fine engravings of famous examples of architecture from all over the world. Oglethorpe was a subscriber to the publication. The book involved great expense, and Castell's artistic taste evidently was greater than his business ability. He was arrested for being in debt and was committed to the Fleet Prison on June 18, 1728.

When the warden discovered that Robert Castell could not pay the bribes he sought, he had him moved to Corbett's Sponging House, which was then infected with smallpox. In spite of many appeals, Castell was kept there, and he soon died.

Oglethorpe visited Castell in prison and was shocked by the conditions which caused his death. He urged an investigation by Parliament into what he felt was a public scandal. He gained the sympathy of some of the most influential members of Parliament, and on February 25, 1729, a committee was appointed to look into the conditions of the prisons of England. James Oglethorpe was its most active member.

During the next few years, Oglethorpe served on many committees. Talk about reform in the prisons continued, and the committees made reports, but more was written about it than was done.

Finally, Oglethorpe succeeded in getting an act passed for the relief of debtors, which set hundreds of them free. Once they were out of prison, however, they were back on the streets of London, unemployed again. Freedom was not the answer to their problems unless some provision was made for their future.

Ideals of the Georgia Colony

Oglethorpe set out to find a solution. On February 13, 1730, he told Sir John Perceval, the first Earl of Egmont, that he had learned of a haberdasher who had left a bequest of £15,000 to be used for charity.

English map showing Georgia located between the Savannah and Altamaha rivers.

Oglethorpe suggested that the money be used to form a trusteeship to obtain land in America, where some of the released debtors might be given a new start. He also hinted that this new colony would grow rapidly and provide raw materials for English industries and would also be a safeguard against the French, Spanish, and Indians to the south of Carolina. They would name the colony Georgia, in honor of King George II.

Lord Egmont agreed, and the idea caught on rapidly. On July 30, 1730, a group of men who called themselves trustees drafted a petition to the king for a grant of lands to the south of Carolina for settling debtors.

Since the southern boundary of South Carolina extended to the Altamaha River, the charter for Georgia stated that the colony of Georgia in America would be that part of South Carolina beginning about 150 miles south of Charles Town at the Rio Dulce, which the English called the Savannah River, and extending south to the Altamaha. The fact that the Lords Proprietors of South Carolina had relinquished their charter to the king in 1729 gave him the right to grant this tract of land to someone else, according to English law, but the South Carolinians insisted for many years afterward that the southern boundary of South Carolina was the Altamaha River.

The trustees, however, made certain that their colony would be entirely separate from South Carolina in its laws, government, and civil economy. The only concession they made was that the governor of South Carolina would control the militia for both colonies.

The king was to receive a quitrent of four shillings for every one hundred acres of land leased by the corporation to their colonists. All land was to be held under feudal law, and no land was to be sold to the colonists. They could only lease it.

On February 6, 1731, Oglethorpe received the good news that the petition had been granted and that he and the other trustees would be responsible for the colonists who went to Georgia for the next twenty-one years. After that time, the government of Georgia was to pass to the king, and it would become a royal colony like South Carolina.

The original trustees were Lord Egmont, who was elected president, Edward Digby, George Carpenter, James Oglethorpe, George Heathcote, Thomas Towers, Robert More, Robert Hucks, Rogers Holland, William Sloper, Francis Eyles, John Laroche, James Vernon, William Belitha, Stephen Hales, John Burton, Richard Bunday, Arthur Bedford, Samuel Smith, Adam Anderson, and Thomas Coram.

Next began much haggling back and forth. More money had to be raised. The petition went back and forth between the trustees and the attorney and solicitor general of the king. After two years of delays, the king signed the charter on April 21, 1732.

Another two months passed before the charter made its way through the channels of government, and it was not until August, 1732, that the trustees could begin their colony.

The charter stated that each man was regarded as both a soldier and a planter. The trustees were to provide him with arms for defense and with tools for cultivation. Towns were to be fortified for the protection of the people. Fifty acres of land were to be leased for each family. Women were not allowed to serve on juries, act as soldiers, or inherit land.

Only Protestants were allowed to enter the colony. Since both the French to the west and the Spaniards to the south were Catholics, Catholics were enemies, and none would be allowed to live in Georgia.

No Slaves or Rum

No Negro slaves were to be owned in Georgia. The reason for this exclusion by the trustees was that the white people who were being sent to the colony had no money with which to purchase slaves if they should be provided. Besides, it was felt by the trustees that, if a white man owned a slave, the white man would do no work, depending on the Negro to do it all.

44

The importation of rum was prohibited, because the trustees knew how much damage was done by drinking spirits in England. A man who got drunk at night did not feel like working the next day, and this caused so much absenteeism in England that they thought to prevent it by prohibiting rum in Georgia. Beer and wine were allowed, however.

The next step was publicity for the colony, of which Oglethorpe was in complete charge. He had to prevent unfriendly articles being published as well as promote positive propaganda. A book was published that upheld the loftiest ideals of the trustees. Though it appeared anonymously, it was generally thought that Oglethorpe had written it.

A design was made for the common seal of the colony of Georgia. On one side were silkworms to show the industry on which the trustees based great hope. Above was the motto *Non sibi sed aliis,* "Not for ourselves but for others." On the reverse side were two men reclining on urns from which flowed the Altamaha and Savannah rivers. In the

The Seal of the trustees from 1733 to 1752 for the new colony of Georgia. The woman, a symbolic figure of Georgia Augusta, wore a cap of liberty and held a spear and a horn of plenty. The two men with urns represented the Savannah and Altamaha Rivers, which were to be the boundaries of Georgia. The silkworm and cocoon showed the hopes of the trustees for the raising of silk, and the motto *Non sibi sed aliis* means "Not for ourselves but for others."

center was a symbolic figure of a woman, Georgia Augusta, wearing a cap of liberty and holding in her hands a spear and a horn of plenty.

The next question was the selection of the first colonists. The trustees inserted a notice in the papers inviting applicants to appear before a committee for examination. Many people responded. In order to be certain of the character of the applicants, a committee was formed to check up on their background.

A few historians maintain that Georgia was first settled by renegades from justice because many of the men were accepted from prison. In fact, this was true of all the colonies, which were used as dumping grounds for criminals. "Transportation" was often the only alternative to hanging at home. Some prisoners, however, were like Oglethorpe's friend, Robert Castell, whose only offense was that they had incurred debts they could not pay, and the trustees' committee carefully examined each transported applicant and accepted or tried to accept only those whose crimes were relatively minor. For this reason, the first colonists to come to Georgia were in many ways superior to the settlers of other colonies who were not so carefully screened.

The final selection for the first embarkation consisted of those who, if in debt, had leave from their creditors to go and were recommended by their minister. By October 3, 1732, 114 persons were ready to embark for Georgia. Each applicant had the charter explained to him, and he signed an agreement of acceptance. When some objected to the statement in the charter that women could not inherit land, it was changed to allow daughters of a family where there was no son to inherit and a widow to inherit one third of her husband's property. At the time of the embarkation, the list had increased to 130 individuals composed of thirty-five families.

An engineer volunteered to go to supervise building a fort, and a doctor offered to attend the sick in Georgia for the first year if a house were built for him and his ground tilled. The Reverend Henry Herbert, D.D., went along as a voluntary chaplain.

Site for Savannah Selected

The trustees chartered the ship *Ann*. She was owned by Samuel Wragg and commanded by John Thomas, who was to sail her to Beaufort, South Carolina. Passage was £4 per head for a minimum of seventy people. Provisions were to be furnished by the trustees, and meals included four beef days, two pork days, and one fish day every week.

The water allowance was one quart per day while the beer lasted and two quarts per day after the beer was gone. The *Ann* was also stocked with medicines, tents, tools, and arms.

Oglethorpe accompanied the colonists at his own expense, and since the charter of the trustees did not designate a governor for Georgia, most of the colonists called Oglethorpe "Father."

The trustees wrote to Governor Robert Johnson of South Carolina for assistance. He donated £50 to the funds of the settlers, and Oglethorpe asked him to apply it to the purchase of provisions in Carolina for the stores of the first settlement. Oglethorpe also asked the governor to hire twenty Negro laborers and four pairs of sawyers to clear the ground on the site he would select.

On November 17, 1732, the settlers and Oglethorpe sailed from Gravesend, England. Several of the trustees were there to see that provisions and accommodations were properly taken care of. The *Ann* stopped at the island of Madeira, where she took on board five tons of wine. Between there and Charles Town, two frail children died at sea, but otherwise the voyage was pleasant. They anchored in Charles Town Harbor on January 13, 1733.

The new colonists found a warm welcome. Although the Carolinians claimed the land, they were glad to have settlers to protect them from the Spanish. Carolina was already sixty-three years old and a mature colony. She feared no rivalry from a small group of settlers who were allowed to have neither slaves nor rum.

Governor Johnson and the assembly had ordered fifteen Rangers to accompany the new settlers as a guard. The scout boat at Port Royal,

South Carolina, was put at Oglethorpe's disposal, small craft were provided to convey the settlers, and a hundred breeding cows, five bulls, twenty sows, four boars, and twenty barrels of rice were given them as a token of goodwill. Colonel William Bull offered to help Oglethorpe find a site and lay out the town.

On January 20, the settlers were transported to Beaufort, where they were housed in the barracks of His Majesty's Independent Company while Oglethorpe and Colonel Bull went ahead to choose a site.

According to the historian Colonel Absalom Chappell, although the Spaniards had named the large river which finally became the northern boundary of their missions the Rio Dulce on their maps, they often called it the Sabana because of the vast expanse of flat land on either side, an area which in Spanish was called *sabana*. The Indians who lived along the river were called the same name by the Spaniards, and the word was spelled in English "Savannah."

Another version of the name "Savannah" says that it was derived from the Shawano or Savannah Indians, a warlike tribe who lived on the western bank of the river near Augusta.

However the name originated, the English had called the river Savannah for many years, and when Oglethorpe and Colonel Bull went up the river to find a site for the new colony of Georgia, Oglethorpe chose Savannah for the name of the first settlement.

A little way up the river they came to Yamacraw Bluff, which rose forty feet above the water. At the north end of the bluff was a village of Yamacraw Indians and a small trading post run by John Musgrove, a Carolinian. Mary Musgrove, his half-Indian wife, spoke both English and the local Indian language. Oglethorpe asked her to be his interpreter, and she introduced him to Tomochichi, the Creek chief, who was about ninety years old.

Little is known of Tomochichi's life up to this time. He told Oglethorpe that he and some of his countrymen of the Yamacraw tribe of Creeks had wandered for many years after the Spaniards deserted Guale.

48

Oglethorpe's interview with Tomochichi.

He was chosen mico of the tribe, and they had returned to their home-land and settled on Yamacraw Bluff shortly before Oglethorpe arrived.

The Indian chief and Oglethorpe liked and respected one another at once and soon became fast friends. Tomochichi had great influence among the Indians and made it possible for the new colonists to keep them as friends.

Friends Help Out

Oglethorpe and Bull returned to Beaufort, and the following Sunday was kept as a Thanksgiving Day. The local people provided a dinner for the new colonists, which included four fat hogs, eight turkeys, fowls, English beef, a hogshead of punch and one of beer, and a con-

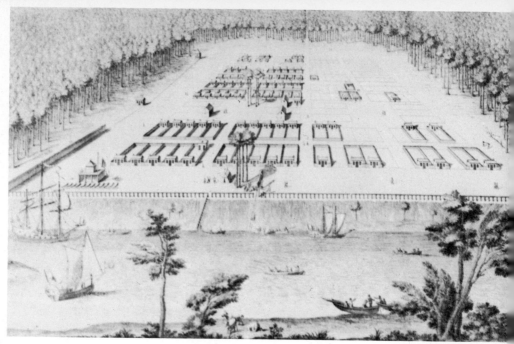

The settlement of Savannah. Oglethorpe had planned the design of the town while still in England.

siderable amount of wine. However, the report of this feast states that no one got drunk.

On January 30, 1733, by their calendar, but February 12 by our present calendar, when a baby in Virginia named George Washington was almost one year old, the colonists finally arrived at the site of Savannah. Four large tents were erected on the edge of a great pine woods for shelter.

Oglethorpe had designed the town in England, and with the help of Colonel Bull, he laid out streets with squares checkerboarded between them. Soon the people began felling the big pine trees for lumber to build their houses.

On February 10, Oglethorpe wrote his first report to the trustees in England. He told them of the help given by persons from South Carolina. To show his appreciation for their help, Oglethorpe named the main street of Savannah for Colonel William Bull. Johnson Square was named for the governor of South Carolina, and Drayton was named for Mrs. Ann Drayton, who lent four sawyers to help with the building. Other streets were named Whitaker, St. Julian, and Bryan, for men from South Carolina who lent slaves or came themselves and worked with the new settlers.

A trust lot was set aside for a church, and Christ Church still occupies that lot today. The Trustees' Garden was laid out and a servant selected to cultivate it. It was to serve as a nursery for trees, vines, and vegetables for the private orchards and gardens of the colonists and was largely devoted to the propagation of mulberry trees.

As the men felled the tall pines and split and sharpened posts with which to stockade the town and to begin the construction of a fort at the eastern end of the bluff, Oglethorpe was present everywhere, planning, supervising, and encouraging. He asked no help for his own shelter. He selected four big pine trees to be left standing, and there he pitched a tent in which he lived for nearly a year.

Fort Argyle

English maps of the coast of Carolina used English names for the rivers and islands. Where Indian names of places were retained, the English spelling differed from the Spanish; Asopo was spelled Ossabaw and Zapala was spelled Sapelo. Santa Catalina became St. Catherine. Later Oglethorpe changed the name of Ospo to Jekyl (now Jekyll) and San Pedro to Cumberland in honor of friends in England. St. Simons Island remained the same.

Although Oglethorpe, with the aid of Mary Musgrove, had obtained the consent of Tomochichi to build the colony on Yamacraw Bluff, he did not feel that this was sufficient. In May, with the help of the Indian chief, he invited fifty Indians, chiefs and braves representing eight of the principal Creek tribes, to come to Savannah. After several days of gift giving, speechmaking, and feasting, a treaty was signed dealing with the ownership of the land and regulating trade.

51

The Creeks agreed to grant to the English all of the land between the Savannah and Altamaha rivers as far west as the tide ebbed and flowed, except for a small place above Yamacraw Bluff where they could make their camp when they visited Savannah. They also kept the islands of Ossabaw, Sapelo, and St. Catherine for hunting, bathing, and fishing. To prevent the Indians from being cheated by traders, a schedule of prices was fixed to set values, such as ten buckskins for one gun, five for a pistol, and one for a blanket.

While the settlers were building their homes and the stockade around the town, the Rangers were stationed just above Yamacraw Bluff for protection. As soon as cannon had been planted and the stockade partially completed, however, Oglethorpe moved part of the Rangers to a place on the Ogeechee River where the Indians crossed. They built a fort which Oglethorpe, in honor of his friend John Campbell, Duke of Argyle (now Argyll), named Fort Argyle. Ten families were sent from Savannah to live near the fort.

Four or five miles south of Savannah, the village of High Gate was laid out, and twelve families moved there. A mile to the east, the village of Hampstead was started with twelve other families. These settlers were to garden and help supply the residents of Savannah with vegetables.

About five miles south of Savannah was a place called Thunderbolt. A letter written by Oglethorpe tells the derivation of the name. A thunderbolt of lightning struck a rock in the area, making a gushing spring whose water smelled like brimstone ever after. A small fort was to be constructed there. Ten families were located on the northwest end of Skidaway Island.

Fifteen miles above the town of Savannah the village of Abercorn was laid out. Four miles below the mouth of Abercorn Creek was Joseph's Town, where Scottish families selected plantations. Nearer Savannah were Sir Francis Bathurst's plantation, Walter Augustin's settlement, and the lands reserved by the Indians just west of Yamacraw.

These outposts were so isolated and malarial fever killed so many of the people that these settlements were eventually abandoned until slave labor was permitted in Georgia.

Near the mouth of the Vernon River at the south end of the Isle of Hope, Dr. Noble Jones built his home, which he named Wormsloe. Jones came to Georgia with Oglethorpe as an officer in charge of a company of English marines. Near Wormsloe he built Fort Wymberley and around it houses in which to quarter the marines who garrisoned the fort. Noble Jones also planted hundreds of mulberry trees with which to feed the silkworms.

A lighthouse, which was to be ninety feet tall, was started on the south end of Tybee Island. Plantations were claimed on Augustine Creek, Wilmington Island, the Isle of Hope, the little Ogeechee at Bewlie, and even as far south as the Great Ogeechee River.

In May, 1733, a ship named the *James* arrived from England with seventeen new colonists sent by the trustees. The ship's captain was awarded the prize which had been offered by the trustees to the first English ship to disembark its cargo at Savannah.

Until July, 1733, Oglethorpe was the sole authority for the colonists. He settled all arguments without a court or jury, and the colonists accepted his decisions as final. As more settlers arrived, however, the task of government became more than he could handle alone.

He held a meeting and appointed magistrates, a recorder, and constables. Thomas Causton was selected to be the keeper of the public stores. A jury was drawn, and a case tried. At noon Oglethorpe provided a dinner for all the colonists. Fresh beef, turkeys, venison, and vegetables from the Trustees' Garden were supplemented by a liberal supply of English beer.

On July 11, 1733, a few days after this meeting, a ship arrived from England with forty Jewish colonists aboard. The trustees had appointed three Jews in England, Alvarro Lopez Sausso, Francis Salvador, Jr., and Anthony Da Costa to solicit contributions for the Georgia colony. They had collected a large sum of money, but instead of turning it over to the trustees, they had recruited forty Jewish colonists, chartered a ship themselves, and set out for Georgia without the approval of the trustees.

Because the trustees had not sent them, Oglethorpe had no power to accept them, but the charter guaranteed freedom of religion to everyone but Catholics, so he decided to let them stay and notified the trustees of their arrival.

With Savannah well on its way, Oglethorpe set out to explore the southern boundary of the province. He left Savannah on the morning of January 23, 1734, with sixteen soldiers and two Indian guides, followed by a yawl loaded with provisions and ammunition. The party landed on St. Simons Island on the evening of the twenty-seventh, and although a hard rain was falling, they camped for the night sheltered by the dense foliage of a large live oak tree with its streamers of Spanish moss.

The next day Oglethorpe decided that a fort should be constructed on St. Simons Island as soon as possible for protection against the Spaniards at St. Augustine. He then went up the Ogeechee River to Fort Argyle and, finding it in good shape, returned to Savannah.

The settlement of Ebenezer, "the Stone of Help."

The German-Speaking Settlers

Back in England, forty-two men with their families who had walked much of the way from their homes in the historic valley of the Salzach River in Austria, waited in London. These people, called Salzburgers, were Lutherans, and they were only a few of the thirty thousand persons who left their homes in Austria because of the persecution of the Protestants by the autocratic archbishops of Salzburg. Like the Huguenots, the Salzburgers had adopted the Protestant religion, and the trustees of Georgia were in sympathy with their beliefs. Even before Oglethorpe had left with the first colonists, he had helped begin arrangements for the Salzburgers to follow him.

Under the leadership of Baron Philip George Frederick von Reck and their religious leaders, the Reverend John Marin Bolzius and Israel Christian Gronau, they arrived at Charles Town on the afternoon of March 7, 1734.

Oglethorpe was in Charles Town on business and sent fresh beef, wine, spring water, cabbages, turnips, radishes, and fruit to the ship as a present from the trustees. Although he had planned to leave for England, Oglethorpe stayed until he had settled the Salzburgers. Since they spoke German, they wanted a town of their own and hoped to find a place like the mountains of Salzburg. This was impossible in coastal Georgia, but Oglethorpe selected for them a site on a crooked, sluggish little creek about four miles below the present town of Springfield in Effingham County and twenty-five miles up the river from Savannah. The Austrians named both the stream and the town Ebenezer, "the Stone of Help."

On Ebenezer Creek, the Salzburgers built their houses, but the ground was constantly flooded from heavy rains, and crops refused to grow.

Tomochichi Visits the King

Now that the colony was a year and three months old and everything seemed to be going well, Oglethorpe decided to visit England. His friend Tomochichi had asked to go with him, and Oglethorpe saw the advantage of showing the Indian to the king and having him entertained at court. He invited Tomochichi and some of the leading members of his tribe to accompany him. The old mico took with him his wife, Senauki, and Tooanahowi, his nephew and adopted son. Hillispylli, the war chief of the Lower Creeks, four of his chiefs, and a Yuchi chief, with their attendants and an interpreter made up the Indian party. They sailed for England on April 7, 1734.

Oglethorpe left the Indians at his estate in the country while he went to London to report to the trustees. After he had conducted his business, he sent three of the king's coaches, each drawn by six horses, to bring the Indian guests to the court. When they were introduced to George II, Tomochichi gave His Majesty several eagle's feathers, the Indians' symbol of highest esteem. Both the king and the mico made long speeches and promised one another respect and friendship.

One of the chiefs was sick and could not attend the presentation. In spite of all the medical care given him, he died. His death disturbed the other Indians, who did not want him to be buried in a strange land. Since he had smallpox, however, it was necessary to bury him immediately. A grave was prepared in St. John's cemetery, Westminster, and the first American Indian chief was buried on English soil.

The Indians were shown all the sights of London. They met the Archbishop of Canterbury and visited Eton College, the Tower of London, Greenwich Hospital, and many public buildings. Tomochichi was much impressed with the riches of the English empire, but he could not understand why short-lived men should want to build such long-lived buildings.

Prince William presented the young mico, John Tooanahowi, with a gold watch, and Tomochichi and his nephew sat for their portraits to be painted.

CHAPTER FOUR

Fort Frederica

After four months in England, Oglethorpe was ready to return to Georgia. He had raised money, selected new colonists, arranged for another group of Salzburgers to return with him, and gathered fortifications for the fort he had received permission to build at Frederica on St. Simons Island.

Tomochichi and the Indians left on the first ship. A group of Scottish Highlanders followed, and toward the end of 1735 Oglethorpe set sail under convoy of a man-of-war, the *Hawk*, commanded by Captain Gascoigne. On board also were John and Charles Wesley, the Salzburgers, a group of Moravians, and other settlers. When the ships

The Highlanders of Scotland are commemorated on a marker in Darien, Georgia. The music of the bagpipes was used for a summons to battle and the accompaniment for funeral processions, as well as for dancing.

docked at Savannah in February of 1736, Oglethorpe was received with a salute of twenty-one guns.

The two hundred Highlanders under Lieutenant Hugh Mackay had already been taken to their new location on the Altamaha River. They named their town Darien and built a fort, a guardhouse, and a chapel. Some of the residents of Savannah had warned them that the Spaniards would attack them, but the Scots replied that they would run the Spaniards out of their own fort and have ready-built houses in which to live.

New Settlers

Another group of persecuted Protestants, German-speaking like the Salzburgers, who found refuge in Georgia were the Moravians. They had fled from Moravia to Saxony under the protection of Count Zinzendorf. The count petitioned the trustees to let the Moravians migrate to Georgia but with the understanding that they should not be required to bear arms or fight because this violated their religion. The trustees unwisely agreed to the condition and the Moravians foolishly accepted.

The Moravians came over not as charity colonists of the trustees but as servants of their patron, Count Zinzendorf, under the provision in the charter that anyone who went to Georgia at his own expense and took ten servants could have a grant of five hundred acres. The count received his grant of five hundred acres on the Ogeechee River. He did not come to Georgia himself, but sent Augustus Gottlieb Spangenberg and nine followers. They landed in Savannah in 1735 and awaited the coming of the Moravians.

Another grant of five hundred acres was secured by Christian, the count's son, and another group of Moravians under the leadership of David Nitschmann, the bishop, left for Georgia on the last day of October, 1735.

When the Moravians arrived, they wanted to be near the Salzburgers because they both spoke German. Instead of accepting the grants on the

Ogeechee River, they settled between Ebenezer and Savannah. They built a schoolhouse named Irene near Tomochichi's village and began to teach the Indian children. Tomochichi was greatly interested in the school and visited it frequently.

The new settlers who were to go to St. Simons Island to make up the colony of Frederica were transferred to small boats and rowed for five days through the waterway between the islands and the mainland. Oglethorpe ordered the food and beer to be put in the forward boats so that no one would lag behind.

All along the way great clumps of moss hung from the trees like eerie masses of gray hair. The Indians told the story of a Spaniard who bought an Indian maid for a wife for a cake of soap and some tarnished braid. The bride was afraid of the old man with his long gray beard and ran away from him and climbed a tree. The Spaniard followed her, and she jumped from the tree into a stream and escaped. The Spaniard's beard became tangled in the branches of the tree, and he could not get loose. He hung there until he died, but his beard lives on in the form of Spanish moss.

Defenses Against the Spanish

As soon as the tents were pitched, Oglethorpe laid out the town of Frederica on a bluff overlooking the inner passage. It was to be a buffer for all the North American colonies against the Spaniards. The town had a military character, with streets named for army officers, a fort, magazine, barracks, entrenchments, and drilling troops. Oglethorpe liked Frederica and made it his home in Georgia rather than Savannah.

Georgia was supposed to extend only as far south as the Altamaha River, but in March, Oglethorpe with Tomochichi, forty Indians, and thirty Highlanders set out to explore the area farther south. Passing Jekyll Island, he landed on the northern end of Cumberland Island, where he left Lieutenant Mackay and the Highlanders to build a fort which he named Fort St. Andrews. Passing the mouth of the St. Marys

Fort Frederica was in 1738 the strongest military fort in North America. It served as a buffer and protection for the English colonies to the north.

River, he named the island there Amelia. The Indians guided the boats to a small island, San Juan, near the mouth of the St. Johns River, where Tomochichi pointed out the castle-fortress of the Spaniards at St. Augustine. The old chief was ready to attack the Spaniards immediately, but Oglethorpe persuaded him to wait.

Since there was no Spanish settlement or fort between the St. Johns River and Frederica, Oglethorpe felt justified in claiming for England everything as far south as San Juan Island. He drew a map showing one of the branches of the Altamaha flowing into the Atlantic Ocean near the St. Marys to prove that Georgia extended at least that far. On the southern end of Cumberland Island, Fort William was built, and on San Juan Island, where the ruins of an old Spanish fort were still visible, Oglethorpe sent a detachment of Highlanders to repair and occupy the old fort. He changed the name of San Juan Island to George and named the fort St. George.

As Georgia grew, Spain began diplomatic protests to England. Oglethorpe had brought from England Charles Dempsey, a commissioner appointed by Parliament, to go to Florida and negotiate with the Spaniards. Dempsey and Major William Richards of Purrysburg left for St. Augustine at the same time Oglethorpe set out on his trip to the mouth of the St. Johns River. They were received by Don Francisco Moral Sanchez, governor of Florida. Sanchez's spies had informed him that Oglethorpe, Tomochichi, and his Indians were on their way and that Captain Gascoigne aboard the man-of-war *Hawk* was in the vicinity.

Suspicious that the English peacemakers were trying to hide the activities of Oglethorpe and the Indians, Sanchez detained Dempsey and Richards until Oglethorpe proved to have no attack in mind.

Oglethorpe Entertains the Spanish Diplomats

The governor of Florida then sent Dempsey and Richards to Captain Gascoigne on the *Hawk*. With them went two Spanish officers who were to inspect the fortifications at Frederica, as Dempsey and Richards had done at St. Augustine. A spy quickly got word to Oglethorpe that the Spaniards were coming, and on June 12, Oglethorpe, with Tomochichi and his Indians in their canoes, started for Fort St. George, which he feared might be attacked. On the way they met the *Hawk*. Oglethorpe sent word to Captain Gascoigne to entertain the Spanish officers until a guard could be furnished because the country was full of Indians who wished to kill them.

As soon as Oglethorpe and Tomochichi could get back from Fort St. George, he sent Lieutenant Mackay to bring some of the Highlanders from Darien. He ordered two handsome tents to be pitched on Jekyll Island. He also sent some refreshments and two messengers to the Spanish commissioners to tell them that he would see them in person the next day.

On the eighteenth, Oglethorpe, with seven mounted men, which were all he had, went to the sea point of St. Simons Island so that the Spaniards could see the men and horses there. Soldiers were drawn up in one long line, to make it seem that there were twice as many as there were. They saluted Oglethorpe with their cannon, reloading and firing some pieces two or three times.

Captain Gascoigne sent a boat for Oglethorpe to go to Jekyll Island, where he talked with the Spanish officers and invited them to dinner the next day aboard the *Hawk*.

The following day, Lieutenant Mackay arrived on board the *Hawk* with his Highlanders. They were dressed in their kilts with bagpipes skirling and were drawn up on one side of the ship while a detachment of the English company in full regimentals lined the other side. The sailors manned the shrouds and kept sentry duty with drawn cutlasses at the cabin door. The Spanish officers were greatly impressed and drank the health of the king of England, and Oglethorpe drank that of the king and queen of Spain.

The next day, Tomochichi, Hillispylli, and thirty Indians came on board painted and dressed as if for war. Hillispylli demanded justice for the Spaniards' killing some of his Indians, but Tomochichi restrained the angry Indians and prevented them from attacking the two Spaniards.

Oglethorpe drew up what he called the Treaty of Frederica, in which it was agreed that neither nation should occupy the mouth of the St. Johns River and that all boundary disputes should be left to the home governments. The Spanish emissaries signed it and took it back to Sanchez, who agreed to it.

The treaty suited the English king well enough, but the Spanish king was so outraged at this apparent surrender by his governor in Florida that he ordered Sanchez home and executed him. He also demanded that the English immediately remove all of their settlements south of the Savannah River, which meant specifically Georgia.

More Money for Troops

As Oglethorpe asked for more and more military support, the trustees called on Parliament for aid. After having fortified the coast almost to

St. Augustine, Oglethorpe went to England on a second visit to secure support for the war with the Spanish, which he knew was inevitable. The trustees asked Parliament to take over the full expense of protecting Georgia.

King George made Oglethorpe a general and commander in chief of all His Majesty's forces in South Carolina and Georgia. He was given permission to raise a regiment to take back with him. So urgent was the situation that a company from the garrison at Gibraltar was sent to Georgia immediately, and in the fall of 1738 Oglethorpe followed with the regiment he had enlisted. Six hundred soldiers with their wives and children on five transports were convoyed by two warships. Spain objected violently and demanded that the English government not allow Oglethorpe to return.

The new troops proved to be almost as much trouble as the Spaniards. Among them were Catholics who sympathized with the Spanish. Before reaching Georgia, Oglethorpe discovered a plot to kill the officers and hand over the regiment to Spain. While inspecting his Gibraltar company, which had been sent to Cumberland Island to strengthen Fort St. Andrews, Oglethorpe was set upon by several soldiers who tried to assassinate him with guns and swords. The ringleader was speedily shot.

After Oglethorpe had restored order to his troops, he set about the task of building roads. The first was built from Frederica to Fort St. Simon. Another was cut from Darien to Savannah, so that no longer were the settlers dependent on transportation by water.

Growth Brings Problems

A messenger came to Oglethorpe asking him to come to Savannah. The Salzburgers at Ebenezer had increased to two hundred, but no matter how hard they worked, they could not prosper. They were discouraged because the creek flooded in winter and dried up in summer.

Pastors Bolzius and Gronau met Oglethorpe in Savannah and asked him to change the location of the town. On February 9, 1736, the three men set out to make an inspection. Oglethorpe tried to persuade the Salzburgers to stay where they were, saying that they had put much time and work into building houses and clearing fields and that they would have to start all over again if they moved. But the Lutherans insisted on abandoning their town, and Oglethorpe finally agreed.

They selected a high ridge on the Savannah River called Red Bluff because of the color of the soil. To it they gave the name of New Ebenezer, and once again they went to work to lay out a town, build houses, and plant crops. Funds received from Germany were used to erect an orphanage, which the settlers also used for a church for several years, until they could afford to build one.

Another matter also claimed Oglethorpe's attention. As early as 1716

Excavations of these houses found the wall foundations of brick and the floors of dry-laid brick set in sand. Fragments of stoneware mugs and medicine bottles show that one building was a tavern and the other an apothecary shop.

This giant oak stands near Christ Church on St. Simons Island where John and Charles Wesley preached to the Indians and organized the first church at Frederica in 1736.

the Carolinians had built a fort and trading post about 150 miles up the Savannah River on the north bank. It was called at different times Fort Moore, Savannah Town, and Adusta, for one of the Indian chiefs of the region. The Upper Creeks and the Cherokees brought furs to this post to be taken to Charles Town. Also, George Galphin was getting rich with his Indian trade at Silver Bluff, a little south of Adusta, and at Galphinton on the Ogeechee River.

Oglethorpe now laid out on the Georgia side of the Savannah River a town which he named Augusta in honor of the Princess of Wales. Every spring hundreds of trappers from the western mountains gathered at Augusta, and it became the center of the fur trade which extended as far west as the Mississippi River.

There were now five principal towns in Georgia: Augusta, Ebenezer, Savannah, Darien, and Frederica. At Frederica the houses were built of tabby, instead of wood, as in most of the other towns. Tabby was a kind of cement made by burning huge piles of oyster shells in order to produce lime. The lime was mixed with sand, shells, and water to make a cement. Forms were built of boards set apart the thickness of a wall to hold the tabby. Only about two feet in height could be poured at one time; then the tabby had to harden for a week or more before the form was moved up and another layer of tabby was poured into it.

Oglethorpe's home at Frederica, which he called the Cottage, was built in the English half-timbered style with heavy exposed framework. On his five hundred acres of land he had an orchard of orange and fig trees and a garden for vegetables. Here he lived for the remainder of the ten years he spent in Georgia.

The Death of a Friend

To maintain friendship with the Indians, Oglethorpe made good use of his interpreter, Mary Musgrove, who invited the Creeks to come to Savannah occasionally to talk with him. In 1738, a group came swearing their allegiance, promising the support of one thousand warriors, if necessary, but also informing Oglethorpe that they had been approached by both Spanish and French agents. A gathering of Creeks, Cherokees, Choctaws, Chickasaws, and others was to take place at Coweta Town on the Chattahoochee River (today the western boundary of the state of Georgia) the next year, and they invited Oglethorpe to be present.

When the time came, Oglethorpe set out on horseback with Indian guides to travel more than two hundred miles through trackless woods and across unbridged streams. He talked to the thousands of Indians gathered at Coweta, settling their grievances against dishonest English traders. By the time the meeting ended, he had made an agreement with the Indians to extend the southern boundary of Georgia to the St. Johns River.

He returned by way of Augusta, where he was told that England had declared war on Spain. After straightening out some misunderstandings with the Cherokees there, Oglethorpe was taken sick with a fever and was in bed for several weeks.

When Oglethorpe reached Savannah, he found the dispatches from England announcing the war between England and Spain. On October 3 he called a meeting of the citizens at the courthouse. The magistrates in their gowns took their places upon the bench, and Oglethorpe sat with them. He told the people that in the present emergency the Indian nations would be their allies. He said that English frigates would cruise along the coast for protection, and land forces were expected from England. The residents of Savannah should be watchful and brave.

Observing that the common was overgrown with bushes and that some of the squares and streets were filled with weeds, the general ordered the entire male population of the town to police duty to clean up the place. Free bread and beer made the task easier.

A few days later the people of Savannah were saddened by the death of Tomochichi. He had been ill for several months, but his mind was clear and active to the end. When he knew that he was near death, he begged his people never to forget the favors he had received from the king when he visited England and to maintain their friendship with the English. He expressed his great love for General Oglethorpe and seemed to have little concern about dying except that it was at a time when his life might have been useful to the English against the Spaniards.

He asked that his body be buried among the English in Savannah, because he had persuaded the Creek Indians to give the land and had assisted in the founding of the town. He died on October 5, 1739, at his own town, four miles north of Savannah at an estimated age of ninety-seven years.

The corpse was brought down the river. Oglethorpe, attended by the magistrates and people of the town, met it at the water's edge. The body was carried to Perceval Square, which is now Wright Square, followed by the Indians and the citizens of Savannah. Minute guns were fired from the battery during the funeral. The general ordered a monument of Georgia granite to be erected over the grave.

The War of Jenkins's Ear

In 1713, through the Treaty of Utrecht at the end of Queen Anne's War, the English had gained the right to supply Spanish colonies with slaves and to send five hundred tons of merchandise annually to Spanish ports. Seldom did the English ships stop at five hundred tons, however, and the Spanish were not always gentle in dealing with Englishmen who tried to smuggle in more than the allotted amount.

Early in 1739, off the coast of Florida, some Spanish inspectors are said to have seized an English smuggler named Thomas Jenkins. They cut off his ear and told him to take it home and show it to his king. Jenkins appeared before Parliament and showed his severed ear to prove how the Spaniards mistreated English traders.

England declared war on Spain in October. Oglethorpe was put in command of the land forces, and the trustees sent Admiral Edward Vernon to command a formidable squadron in the West Indies. Serving under the admiral at the ill-fated siege of Cartagena, New Granada (now Colombia), in 1741, was young Lawrence Washington of Virginia, George's half brother. Washington so admired Admiral Vernon that he named his estate in his honor, and Mount Vernon it remains to this day.

The trustees had sent no funds or supplies to Georgia, and since the withdrawal of the Highlanders from the outpost on St. Simons Island in 1736, the small fort on Amelia was the most southern point fortified. After burying Tomochichi, Oglethorpe began to prepare the colony for war. He could count on about two hundred fighting men to be recruited in Georgia. He asked Mary Musgrove to rouse the Indians and sent runners to the Creek country to call for a thousand warriors. He himself set out for Frederica.

As rumors about Spaniards marching against Savannah grew, there

68

was more drilling of the militia, and a census was taken of those who could be classed as fighters. The Moravians not only refused to march back and forth with guns in their hands, but they also refused to be counted, reminding the English that the trustees had promised that they would not have to fight.

Feelings against them became bitter, and there were threats that the Moravians would be killed if they did not help. After drawing lots, which was their way of making a decision, they decided to go to Pennsylvania, where there was another colony of Moravians. The other Savannah people, however, refused to let them go until they had paid all debts they owed. A few at a time, as the debts were reduced, they left, and by the middle of 1740 all of them had gone.

The Spaniards attacked first. They fell upon the Highlanders on Amelia Island, killed two of them, and hacked their bodies to pieces. Quickly retaliating, Oglethorpe led a company of troops as far south at the mouth of the St. Johns River, where he searched the countryside but could find no Spaniards.

Lieutenant George Dunbar went up the river to attack two Spanish forts, Picolata and St. Francis, but finding them strongly fortified and having no artillery, he withdrew. Oglethorpe, with the Highlanders and some Indians in fifteen boats, made an attack on these forts on New Year's Day of 1740 and took both of them.

Having cleared the way, Oglethorpe planned an advance on St. Augustine. Now that he had been appointed commander in chief of the royal forces in both South Carolina and Georgia, he went to Charles Town to ask for aid. Though the residents of South Carolina had been enthusiastic at the founding of Georgia for their own protection, the colony had grown so rapidly and Oglethorpe had been so successful in getting aid from England that the Carolinians had become jealous. After much haggling, Oglethorpe was given a regiment of five hundred men and a promise of one hundred more. The prospect of looting and plunder was largely responsible for their going at all.

By the late spring of 1740, Oglethorpe was able to collect nine hundred regulars and provincial troops and eleven hundred Indians with which to invade Florida. Oglethorpe took his forces by water, and the Highlanders marched across country. When they arrived at Fort Moosa, two miles from St. Augustine, the Spaniards evacuated it and retired into the castle-fortress. Because of the shallow water of the bar and the presence of Spanish galleys, the English fleet was unable to attack.

With his plans all awry, Oglethorpe settled down to a siege, hoping to starve out the garrison, but the Spanish fleet was able to get into the harbor and relieve the fort, and a detachment of Spaniards slipped out and killed the Highlanders who had taken Fort Moosa. There was nothing for Oglethorpe to do but retreat.

The Georgians blamed the South Carolinians for failure to play their part in the expedition, and the South Carolinians charged Oglethorpe with incompetence. Oglethorpe marched back north with his sick, dispirited troops, and at Frederica he himself lay sick with fever for the next two months.

Convinced that the Spanish were preparing to make an all-out attack on Georgia to destroy her, the general tried in every way to get help. The trustees ignored his pleas, however, and he was left to his own resources. He strengthened the string of forts down the coast, maintained good relations with the Indians, and in desperation asked South Carolina for more troops. The South Carolinians refused, and Oglethorpe was left alone in Georgia to meet the Spaniards.

The Battle of Bloody Marsh

In the early summer the Spaniards collected an army and fleet in Havana, sailed for St. Augustine, and proceeded up the coast in fifty vessels with eighteen hundred soldiers and one thousand seamen. They headed straight for Fort Frederica, and on July 4, 1742, they stood off St. Simons Sound preparing to land on the island.

70

The Battle of Bloody Marsh has been called one of the fifteen decisive battles of history. Here, 652 British soldiers ambushed the Spanish army of 4,000 soldiers and drove them into the marsh, which ran red with blood.

They ran by Fort St. Simon without difficulty and landed a few miles up the inner passage toward Frederica. To prevent being cut off and captured, the garrison in Fort St. Simon spiked their guns and retreated. The Spaniards marched in, took possession of the fort, and prepared to follow the retreating Georgians to Frederica. The road which the Georgia regiment had built from Fort St. Simon to Frederica became the center of Oglethorpe's strategy.

Captain Noble Jones, with a detachment of regulars and Indians, was sent on a scouting party. He met a small detachment of the enemy's advance troops who did not know that they were so far ahead of the main body. They were surprised and taken prisoner. From them it was learned that the whole Spanish army was advancing. The information was sent by an Indian runner to General Oglethorpe.

A force of 170 Spanish regulars and Indians marched up the road to within a mile of Frederica. Before they were able to clear the woods and deploy in the open savannah, Oglethorpe attacked with his Rangers and Highlanders. They captured the commander and killed or captured most of the force. The remnant retreated, followed by the English.

The Georgians concealed themselves in some trees on the edge of an open glade while Oglethorpe returned to Frederica to bring reinforcements. Another Spanish detachment arrived, discovered the Georgians, and put them to flight. Some of the Highlanders, however, executed a flank movement around the Spaniards and prepared an ambush in some trees on the edge of a marsh about two miles from Fort St. Simon.

A large body of Spaniards marched into the marsh, stacked their arms, made fires, and were preparing their kettles for cooking when a horse was frightened by some movement of the British in ambush and began to snort. The Spaniards ran to their arms, but before they could form and fire, they were shot down by the Scots, who remained hidden in the trees. After repeated attempts to form, the Spaniards fled, leaving their camp equipage on the field. They did not stop until they got under cover of the guns on their ships.

Many left without their arms; others discharged their muskets over their shoulders while retreating. The Spaniards fired so much at random that the trees were denuded by the balls from their muskets. Their loss in dead, wounded, and prisoners was estimated at five hundred. Before leaving the island, the Spaniards destroyed the town and fort of St. Simon.

This engagement came to be known as the Battle of Bloody Marsh. It was a major defeat for the Spaniards, causing their main force to return to Florida and preventing another attack on Georgia.

Oglethorpe Leaves Georgia

Now that he had driven the Spaniards from the coast of Georgia, Oglethorpe received letters of congratulation from the governors of

New York, New Jersey, Pennsylvania, Maryland, Virginia, and North Carolina. The governor of South Carolina did not join in these thanks, but the people of Port Royal, South Carolina, did, much to the governor's chagrin.

In March of 1743, Oglethorpe once more went to St. Augustine, but the Spanish refused to come out of their castle-fort and fight. Oglethorpe never again bothered the Floridians.

Although Oglethorpe was one of the most popular and best-loved colonial leaders in America, there were men who did their best to destroy him. One of these, a lieutenant colonel of Oglethorpe's regiment, made serious charges against the general concerning false promises of payment to officers. Oglethorpe returned to England on June 23, 1743, to face the charges of a court-martial, but he was acquitted.

The defense of the colony was left in the hands of Major William Horton at Frederica, and William Stephens was made deputy-general of Georgia in Savannah.

Oglethorpe had spent ten years in Georgia, leading the colony to victory against the strongest forces the Spaniards could launch against it. During this time he had paid out more than £12,000 for the expenses of his regiment and the colony from his own pocket, without any promise of its being refunded. Although he lived to see Georgia become an independent state and part of a greater independent nation, he never visited her again.

Years later he was offered the governorship of South Carolina but refused it. When the Revolutionary War began in America, General Oglethorpe was senior general of the British army, and when General Thomas Gage was recalled from America, Oglethorpe was asked to accept the position of commander in chief in America. He declined the honor, and the command was given to Sir William Howe.

CHAPTER FIVE

Life Without Slaves or Rum

Although Englishmen had never been interested in producing silk in England, the trustees had early decided that it should be the main industry in Georgia. They did not doubt that, because the settlers would receive free passage, land, and mulberry trees, they would be willing to do whatever the trustees wanted in gratitude.

England bought 500,000 pounds of silk a year from Italy and France. Georgia was expected to produce more than that, giving employment to twenty thousand colonists and also providing the raw materials for twenty thousand workers in England, who made consumer goods from it.

Oglethorpe was skeptical about making Georgia into a mulberry forest, and he was much more interested in the military possibilities of the colony than the commercial, but he carried out the rules and saw to it that mulberry trees were planted and silk raising was taught.

Cloth from a Worm

Making silk is a long and tedious job. First the moth lays eggs, from which caterpillars will hatch, which feed on the leaves of the mulberry tree. One caterpillar eats thousands of such leaves during its lifetime.

The silk-producing organs of the caterpillar consist of two large glands containing a viscid substance. They extend throughout the body and end in two outlets called seripositors near the mouth. After about eight weeks of leaf eating, the caterpillar stops eating and begins the task of spinning the silk. When the cocoon is finished, the threads are double, one coming from each of the caterpillar's two silk-producing organs. The cocoon is about the size of a pigeon's egg, and the double thread often is more than a thousand feet long. It takes the caterpillar about five days to spin the cocoon, after which two or three weeks elapse before the moth eats its way out of the cocoon and lays eggs to repeat the process.

However, if the moth is allowed to come out, the threads will break. The silkworm grower prevents this by putting all the cocoons, except those which he intends to keep for breeding, into hot water or an oven heated by hot air or steam, to kill the worms inside the cocoons before they turn into moths. The breeding cocoons are selected with care, so that there will be an equal number of male and female insects, the females being known in the chrysalis stage by their larger size.

The cocoons intended for the production of moths are placed on a cloth in a darkened room, where the temperature is kept near 72 degrees. When they hatch, the moths show no inclination to fly away but remain on the cloth, lay their eggs, and die there. The caterpillars remain contentedly in the boxes or trays in which they are placed, feeding on leaves provided for them until ready to spin their cocoons.

After the heat kills the caterpillars, the cocoons are placed in basins of warm water to soften the natural gum which coats the silk threads. The operator takes a small brush made of twigs and stirs the water. This catches the outside strands of silk and starts the unwinding process. From three to five strands of silk are twisted into one thread and pass through a polished metal or glass eye in the reeling machine, or filature, which reels the raw silk into hanks. Each cocoon yields about three hundred yards of thread. If a thread breaks or a cocoon runs out, another thread is joined to make the thread the same size all the way.

The raw silk is washed in warm, soapy water to remove the gum. Then the threads are twisted into various sizes, to be used for the warp or weft of the cloth woven from it.

A large building for producing the silk, also called a filature, was built in Savannah. The trustees hired Paul Amatis from the Piedmont section of Italy to come to Georgia with the first settlers on the *Ann* to teach the English colonists how to raise silk. He was followed by his brother, Nicholas Amatis, and his helpers, Mr. and Mrs. Jacob Camus and their children. The Amatis brothers quarreled and moved to South Carolina in 1736, and the Camuses took over the instruction at a salary of £60 a year plus a free house and garden. Mrs. Camus grew jealous of some of her better pupils, however, and in 1750 she and her family also moved to South Carolina.

The Salzburgers soon became the chief silkworm producers in the colony, supplying more than half of all the cocoons sent to the filature in Savannah. The first amount which they produced was taken to England by Oglethorpe on his first trip, and it attracted so much attention that Queen Caroline, wife of King George II, had it made into a dress which she wore to court on her birthday. In 1750 the Salzburgers produced over one thousand pounds of cocoons. In 1764, more than fifteen thousand pounds of silk were produced at the filature, over half of which had been raised by the Salzburgers.

About this time the silk business in Georgia reached its climax; thereafter it steadily declined. It was deserted by the colonists for more lucrative pursuits, such as raising tobacco and rice.

Music and Dancing

As Savannah grew, the social life began to take shape. Since most of the colonists had had no money or possessions when they left England, they brought nothing with them in the way of household goods. But several people brought with them their violins, or fiddles, as they were then called.

When William Stephens was put in charge of the colony with the title of president, he kept an account of events in a journal which was later published. Here he told of how, after Mary Musgrove's husband died, she and Thomas Bosomworth were married. Although Bosomworth was a minister, he thought it proper to have dancing at their wedding reception, but no one had a house large enough to accommodate all the colonists they wanted to invite. They asked William Stephens, who was living in one of the trustees' houses, if they might use it. He moved his furniture and let them use the front rooms for dancing. A fiddler provided the music.

At a time when the ministers of New England were trying to destroy the evils of dancing, a minister in Georgia invited his parishioners to dance at his wedding reception.

The earliest settlers, mostly of the Church of England, brought with them religious books, including psalters, or hymnbooks. The Salzburgers and Moravians had their own religious music, too.

The music of the Highlanders at Darien must have seemed strange to the other colonists. In their kilts they paraded on the river bluff in view of scouting parties of Spaniards. The weird sound of skirling bagpipes expressed the Scots' defiance of the raiders.

The bagpipes were also used by the Scots as a summons to battle, an accompaniment for a funeral procession, or as music for dancing. The other colonists in Savannah danced the stately steps of the minuet, but the Scots with their pipes danced the Highland fling and the lively reel.

In 1752, a whole community moved from Dorchester, South Carolina, to settle at Midway, Georgia. They were Congregationalists, originally from Dorchester, Massachusetts. With the people already living at Midway they formed the Midway Church in August, 1754.

The Dorchester people liked to sing church music and paid their choristers. Separate seats were used by the choir, who sang many of the early tunes in parts. Parmenas Way was the director, and he set the pitch with the aid of a tuning fork which is now on display in the Midway Museum.

The Men of Strict Methods

John Wesley was born on June 17, 1703, in Epworth Rectory, Lincolnshire, England, where his father was the rector. Four years later, on December 18, 1707, his brother Charles was born. Both brothers went to school at Christ Church, Oxford. John decided to become a minister and was ordained deacon in 1725 and became a priest in 1728. He left Oxford in 1727 to help his father, but returned in 1729 as a tutor.

During John's absence, Charles and two other young men began to exhibit an almost fanatical religious fervor. Because they lived by such strict methods, one young man of Christ Church exclaimed that they had started a new sect—Methodism. Many years after, John Wesley defined a Methodist as one who arranged his life according to the method laid down in the New Testament. John and Charles Wesley, John Ingham, and George Whitefield met regularly in spite of the ridicule they received.

John and Charles were asked by the trustees to go to Georgia with Oglethorpe on his second trip. John was to take the place of the Reverend Samuel Quincy, the minister in Savannah who had been dismissed by the trustees because of complaints by the colonists. Charles was to be Oglethorpe's secretary.

The Wesleys sailed on the *Symond* along with the Reverend Benjamin Ingham and Charles Delamotte, the son of a London merchant and friend of the Wesleys. Among the passengers were twenty-six Moravians, who made a strong impression on the Wesleys. John was so eager to talk with them that he began to study German. During a storm the Moravians showed no fear of shipwreck, and John was moved by their courage.

On Sunday, February 14, 1736, the vessel landed. With his fellow passengers around him, John Wesley prayed for the first time in the New World, giving thanks for the safe voyage.

78

The Wesley brothers. Charles Wesley (left), younger brother of John, is best remembered as a writer of hymns. John Wesley, who started the world's first Sunday School in Savannah, was the founder of Methodism.

Charles accompanied Oglethorpe to Frederica. The town had no minister, and Charles was expected to take spiritual charge as well as act as Oglethorpe's secretary. But Charles was not able to carry out the responsibilities of the work. He thought the people did not take their spiritual obligations seriously, and by the end of the first month he had quarreled with several of them.

He found his duties as Oglethorpe's secretary a burden. His congregation shrank to two Presbyterians and a Catholic. The poorly built houses in the cold, damp climate kept him sick with a cold or fever the whole time he was there.

John visited his brother in Frederica, and because there was no church, he preached under a large oak tree. He had hoped that his visit

Charles Wesley preaches under a spreading oak. The Wesley brothers came to Georgia with great hopes of converting the Indians to Christianity.

would help Charles, but it did not seem to do so. John suggested that he and Charles change places for a while, and Charles seemed to be happier in Savannah. He did not like Georgia, however, and on July 26, 1736, only five months after he arrived, Charles left Savannah to return to England. In a friendly parting with him, Oglethorpe advised Charles to get married, suggesting that if he had a wife to take care of him, he would be a better minister.

John and Charles loved singing with their services, and Charles was a gifted poet. He wrote many hymns, including "Jesus, Lover of My Soul," "Love Divine, All Loves Excelling," "Christ the Lord Is Risen To-day," and "Hark! the Herald Angels Sing." John collected a small volume of seventy-two pages called *A Collection of Psalms and Hymns*, which he had published by Timothy Lewis in Charles Town in 1737.

Both the Wesleys worked as members of the Church of England when in Georgia, but the idea of Methodism was in their minds. John later dated the beginning of Methodism as 1729, when the four men met together at Oxford.

An Unhappy Love Affair

John Wesley started the first Sunday School in Savannah in the parish of Christ Church, nearly fifty years before Robert Raikes began his Sunday School in Gloucester, England, and eighty years before a Sunday School was established in any other colony. The Sunday School begun by Wesley was continued by George Whitefield at the orphanage of Bethesda and has existed until the present, making it the oldest Sunday School in the world.

John worked hard in Savannah. Every Sunday and holiday he administered the Lord's Supper. On weekdays he read prayers at five o'clock in the morning and at seven in the evening. The colonists did not like these High Church practices, and when Wesley made a mistake in his personal life, they used it as an excuse to condemn him.

Thomas Causton, the storekeeper, had an attractive niece named Sophia Christina Hopkey. Sophia was a devoted attendant at church services and flirted continuously with the handsome young preacher, even asking him to give her French lessons. Wesley's friend, Charles Delamotte, regarded Sophia as sly and designing and doubted her sincerity. He warned John against her.

Wesley was so attracted to Sophia that he discussed the matter of marrying her with his friends, the Moravians. They also advised him against her, and Wesley began to see less of the young lady.

Sophia was angry at the change in John and turned her attention to another suitor named Williamson, whom she soon married. But as her spiritual adviser, Wesley continued to visit Sophia after she was married. As Sophia grew less and less attentive to church duties, Wesley decided it was his duty to deny her Holy Communion.

This act enraged both the husband and uncle of the lady. They sued Wesley in the civil court for defamation of Sophia's character, and in the public quarrel which followed, the people took sides against the minister. Wesley refused to accept the suit, saying that the civil court had no authority over him because he was a minister. A warrant was issued for his arrest, and to avoid further trouble he decided to go back to England.

One year and nine months after he had arrived, John Wesley left Savannah secretly by night in the company of a bankrupt constable, a ne'er-do-well wife beater, and a defaulting barber. They rowed up the river to the Swiss settlement at Purrysburg and began to walk toward Beaufort, South Carolina. They lost the way and wandered about in a swamp for a whole day with no food but a piece of gingerbread.

Finally, they arrived at Beaufort, where Charles Delamotte joined them, and they took a boat to Charles Town. Here Wesley preached

James Habersham, who came to Georgia with George Whitefield to help build Bethesda Orphanage. This portrait was painted by Jeremiah Theus, who lived in Charles Town.

George Whitefield, whose eloquent oratory raised money for Bethesda Orphanage, where as many as 150 orphans were cared for.

once more and four days later left America on the *Samuel*. Wesley was disappointed most of all in himself and blamed no one else for his failure in Georgia.

House of Mercy

Before he decided to leave Georgia, John Wesley had written several letters to his old friend from Oxford days, George Whitefield. Whitefield was one of the most fabulously eloquent preachers the church ever produced. Ordinary pastors were jealous of him and barred him from their pulpits, so he took to preaching in the open fields, chiefly to the coal miners of Bristol. He knew that he had moved them when he began to see white tracks crawl down their black faces—the marks of tears.

John wanted Whitefield to come to Georgia and help him build an orphanage. Whitefield and James Habersham were on a boat leaving London when John Wesley returned. Wesley sent word to Whitefield that he had better stay in England, but Whitefield and Habersham went on to Georgia.

The two men selected a site for an orphanage about twelve miles from Savannah. This was the first orphanage in America, and they named it Bethesda, meaning House of Mercy, because they hoped it would be a house of mercy for many children.

Whitefield spent a great deal of effort building Bethesda. He made voyages back and forth to England and traveled up and down the American colonies, preaching to large congregations, often on open hillsides or in public halls, to raise money for his project. He collected large sums of money from rich and poor alike with his eloquent appeals.

Benjamin Franklin told of attending one of Whitefield's sermons. He saw immediately that the speaker intended to finish with a collection. The printer had in his pocket a handful of copper coins, three or four silver dollars, and five pistoles of gold, but he firmly resolved that he would contribute nothing to Whitefield's cause.

As the speaker proceeded, Franklin was impressed by his oratory and decided to contribute the copper coins. A few minutes later he grew ashamed to give so little, and he thought he would give the silver. But by the time Whitefield had finished, Franklin emptied his pocket into the collection plate, gold and all.

For nineteen years Whitefield worked for Bethesda, building first a main building to which two wings, each 150 feet long, were added. Eventually the orphanage became Bethesda College. When he felt that his life was near an end, Whitefield willed the property to the Right Honorable Selina, Countess of Huntingdon, a distant relative of George Washington, who had befriended him, paid his debts, and once appointed him her chaplain. Whitefield stated in his will that, if she should die, it was to go to James Habersham, who had opened a large trading business in Savannah.

The right Honorable Selina, Countess of Huntingdon, England. When George Whitefield willed her the orphanage, she had this full-length portrait painted by Sir Joshua Reynolds and sent it to Bethesda. It now hangs in Hodgson Hall at the Georgia Historical Society in Savannah.

When the will was read, Lady Huntingdon set apart a day for fasting and prayer. She had hardly begun to take over the work, however, when lightning struck the buildings, and they were destroyed by fire. Lady Huntingdon spent her own money to restore the buildings, but the work was interrupted by the outbreak of the Revolutionary War. She sent to Bethesda a full-length portrait of herself painted by Sir Joshua Reynolds, which today hangs in Hodgson Hall of the Georgia Historical Society in Savannah.

There was, however, one critic of Bethesda. An Englishman who visited the orphanage several times said in his journal in 1740 that he thought there was too much praying and singing of hymns and that the discipline was too strict. The children were not allowed a minute of recreation or time to play.

The Bible As Textbook

The trustees left the matter of establishing schools to the Georgians. One of the first schools was Irene, where the Moravians began teaching Indian children in 1735. The Reverend Benjamin Ingham taught there for two years, learned the Indian language, and began writing a Creek grammar.

In Savannah, Charles Delamotte, Wesley's friend, started a school where he charged tuition and where he not only taught the children to read, write, and do sums but also instructed them in the catechism. After Delamotte went back to England with John Wesley, John Dobell continued the school, which was later made free to all. In a letter dated June 11, 1742, Dobell requested supplies from the trustees, among which were six psalmbooks by Tate and Brady. The Bible was used as a textbook, as was the custom in all colonial schools.

Art did not flourish in Georgia, and there was no well-known artist in the colony. However, Jeremiah Theus lived in Charles Town, and a letter from James Habersham to him, dated July 31, 1772, states that Habersham had received all his family portraits as well as those of several other members of the community. Theus had come to Savannah and painted the faces of the subjects. Then he took the unfinished canvases home to paint the clothes and backgrounds. He charged £320 for the seven portraits of the Habersham family members.

A Rum-Selling Doctor

Dr. Patrick Tailfer was a pharmacist and surgeon who came to Georgia among the first colonists. He found that there was more money in selling rum illegally than there was in selling pills. He was the leader of a group of Scots who wanted to make both rum and slaves legal.

They met nightly at Jenkins Tavern, wrote demanding letters to Oglethorpe, and posted anonymous protests in the public square.

Tailfer promoted horse racing and betting and was chairman of the group who formed the Free Mason Club. They insisted that law in England was not law in Georgia and that the trustees should encourage the manufacture of goods in Georgia.

Tailfer did not last long. When the Spanish attacked Amelia Island in 1739, he appointed himself captain of a company to defend Savannah, but he became frightened, left his business affairs in the hands of a potter, and fled to Charles Town.

Just before the Revolution started, the outstanding physician in Savannah was Dr. Noble Wymberley Jones, son of Dr. Noble Jones, who was one of the original settlers. At his home, Wormsloe, on the Isle of Hope, Noble Wymberley Jones learned the practice of medicine from his father. At the beginning of the Revolution, his father's illness prevented Wymberley from attending the Continental Congress. Otherwise he would have been a signer of the Declaration of Independence.

CHAPTER SIX

Political Independence

While Oglethorpe was in charge of Georgia, he settled any disputes that arose among the colonists. When it had been discovered that Thomas Causton, the storekeeper for the colony, had been cheating the trustees for several years, Oglethorpe was the one who reported it to the trustees and executed their orders to have him arrested and sent to England for trial. After Oglethorpe left, however, the local government was not strong enough to maintain the trustees' laws.

Colonel William Stephens was appointed deputy general of the colony, but still no provision was made for a governor. The three laws passed by the trustees before the founding of Georgia, prohibiting the importation of rum and slaves and the ownership of land, began to irritate the colonists more and more. South Carolinians were becoming wealthy raising rice with slave labor and selling rum illegally to the Georgians.

From the trustees' standpoint, Georgia was to be an ideal colony even to the extent of not needing lawyers, who were forbidden to practice in the colony. But as in the case of Causton, men broke the laws and needed to be tried in Georgia rather than to be sent back to England.

The Colonists' Complaints

The colony was to be a religious haven except for Catholics, but John and Charles Wesley angered the people with their strict religious discipline. Men were to stay sober without any liquor stronger than beer or wine, but they wanted to drink rum, gin, or brandy as their South Carolina neighbors did, and soon rum-running became a lucrative business. Grogshops were opened publicly, and when those who sold hard liquor were arrested, no jury could be found to convict them. Even the magistrates drank rum and were unwilling to prosecute anyone else for that offense.

After ten years the colonists were disillusioned, and they blamed the trustees for all their complaints. No one seemed to be prospering; the land was too sandy to be fertile; little silk was raised; rice and corn were grown only in small amounts; the olive trees died and all the exotic plants which the trustees' garden was to provide withered. Malarial fever was prevalent, and the sun was hot; few new settlers came to the colony, and many were leaving. The people did not want to work on land that was not theirs; they did not like to plant mulberry trees, and they wanted more rights in the government.

The demand for slaves grew louder. Those who wanted to plant rice could not do so without the help of slaves. This fight centered in Savannah. The Salzburgers, who had never seen a black man in their European home, feared the Negroes and opposed the use of slaves. The Highlanders also objected to slaves, saying that no one had the right to own another person.

Many Georgians, without waiting for the law to be changed, began to rent black people from their South Carolina owners. If they were threatened by exposure, they would return the slaves to the owners in South Carolina. As renting became more successful, instead of renting black men for a few years, they hired them for a hundred years and paid the owner the full price.

The grumblers circulated a petition which was signed by 121 Savannah citizens. They demanded rum, slaves, and ownership of land. The trustees could not understand such ingratitude and promptly refused the demands and dismissed the magistrates who had signed it.

Next, the protesters decided to ignore the trustees and approach the government directly. They sent Thomas Stephens, son of William Stephens, the deputy general, to England to lay the demands before Parliament. The elderly William Stephens did not approve of his son's errand, nor did Parliament. They upheld the trustees, and as a measure of humiliation, they forced Thomas to kneel and receive a reprimand from the House.

As the years passed and the demands grew stronger, the trustees began to relent. First they withdrew the law against rum. By 1748, men like George Whitefield, James Habersham, and even the Salzburgers advised the trustees to admit slaves. The next year the trustees agreed, but slaves were to be allowed in a limited form, and strict rules regulated slave ownership. For every four black slaves, the owner must have one white male bondsman. He must register his slaves in the Colonial Records, teach them the responsibilities of marriage, and allow no marriages with whites. Slaves must not be made to work on the Lord's Day, and they must attend Christian church service.

Slavery immediately spread throughout the colony.

Also disregarding the trustees' laws about land, many people in Georgia claimed estates far beyond the fifty acres allowed, some holding lease on as much as two thousand acres. In 1750 the land laws were removed, and the people were permitted to buy and sell land as they pleased.

Empress Mary Musgrove

Mary Musgrove's husband, Thomas Bosomworth, had been sent to Georgia as a minister and for a while had performed his duties regularly, but he saw an opportunity to take advantage of Mary's position with the Creek Indians. He induced them to grant to him and Mary the three islands—St. Catherine, Ossabaw, and Sapelo—they had reserved when they made the land treaty with Oglethorpe. Next, he talked the Creeks into declaring Mary their empress and told them how the English had

Although Mary Musgrove, a half-breed Indian, had been a good friend to Oglethorpe, her third husband, Thomas Bosomworth, persuaded her to demand from the English all the land formerly belonging to the Creeks. Mary proclaimed herself their empress, and with an army of Indians marched on Savannah to make her demands.

stolen their land. In 1749 he and Mary led a menacing army of Indians to the outskirts of Savannah to force the colony to pay him the salary which Oglethorpe had promised Mary but which Bosomworth claimed had never been paid.

President Stephens ordered out the militia, and Captain Noble Jones, with a troop of mounted men, commanded the Indians to ground their arms, declaring that no armed Indian was allowed in the town.

The Indians reluctantly laid down their arms. When they entered the town, the citizens were terrified, and all sorts of rumors abounded. The Indians, having been roused to the point of war, demanded that the whites leave all lands lying south of the Savannah River, threatening that if they refused, every settlement within those limits would be burned to the ground.

The following day, Bosomworth was arrested, and Mary continued to demand that every white person in Savannah leave her country. Finally, President Stephens ordered Mary to be put in jail with her husband, so that the Georgians could talk with the Indian chiefs. They learned that Bosomworth was badly in debt and wanted to get the Indians' lands so that he could sell them and pay his creditors in South Carolina.

President Stephens distributed presents among the Indian chiefs, and Mary was turned loose. But in the council room she ordered the Indians to attack the whites. Noble Jones dispersed the Indians, and Mary and Bosomworth were kept in jail until they agreed to cause no more trouble.

The Bosomworths carried their fight to the courts for the next ten years both in Georgia and in England. Finally they gained a settlement which gave them St. Catherine Island, where they lived, and the sum of £2,100.

The Trustees Give Up Georgia

The trustees had been so intent on the social experiment in Georgia that they had neglected its governmental needs. They did not learn until the last year of their control over the colony that they should give the people governmental power.

Georgia had only a general court of three judges, called bailiffs, and a recorder. But though the government was small, there were duties for it to perform. People quarreled and fought and got into debt again and were thrown into prison even in this land which was to abolish debt. Still, however, there were no lawyers.

The year before the Georgia charter was to expire, the trustees decided to let the Georgians have a little more self-government. They were afraid that South Carolina, which had already begun to show signs of wanting to get back the land that once had been hers, would have less chance of annexing Georgia if Georgians were granted stronger local government.

An assembly was called in Savannah in 1751. It was attended by delegates from every town and settlement in the colony as large as ten families. The assembly could not pass laws, but it did make suggestions to the trustees and discussed complaints of the colonists. The assembly recommended to the trustees that Savannah should have a new wharf and that ships should not dump ballast into the river. They also asked that the charter be renewed to prevent South Carolina's annexing the colony and that the people be given the right to make their own laws and to organize a militia.

Although the trustees did not accept all the recommendations, they were pleased with this first experiment in self-government. They agreed that the assembly should meet again the next year but stated that no one should serve in it who did not have one hundred mulberry trees and produce fifteen pounds of silk a year on each fifty acres of land he possessed.

The trustees approved the recommendation of the assembly to organize the militia. Any man owning three hundred acres of land was made a cavalryman and was required to appear mounted at each muster. All other able-bodied men belonged to the infantry. In June, 1751, the first military review was held in Savannah; about 220 infantrymen paraded, with Noble Jones as commander. Since Oglethorpe's regiment had been disbanded, the defense of the colony was now in its own hands, and the militia was important.

As was their custom, the trustees asked Parliament in 1751 for an appropriation to help maintain Georgia. Having already done much more for Georgia than it had ever done for any other American colony, Parliament refused to give further help. The king was asked for aid, but he too answered that Georgia should get no further help until the trustees gave up their charter. As the trustees had only one more year of official life left, they agreed to give up their charter at once, surrendering it on June 23, 1752.

The Georgians were afraid that the king might not give them as good a government as the trustees had or that South Carolina might swallow up the colony. Before the trustees surrendered their rights to Georgia, however, they secured the king's promise of a separate colonial government for Georgia.

CHAPTER SEVEN

A Royal Province

K ing George II had had enough trouble with liberal American colonies like Pennsylvania and Maryland and self-governing colonies like Rhode Island and Connecticut. Georgia would be a royal province like Virginia or New York, and the king would rule it as he pleased.

In April, 1751, a committee was appointed to decide the status of the colony. It recommended that Georgia be made a royal province, separate and independent, and that the land owned by the colonists remain in title as granted to them under the trustees' charter. Instead of being called a colony, Georgia was called a province and had the same kind of government as any other royal province, with a governor appointed by the king and an assembly elected by the people. A province had a higher governmental status than a colony and its officials had more authority. It was, thus, a matter of pride to be a province rather than a colony.

As usual, the clever, the aggressive, and the strong gradually took over the local government to make it serve their selfish ambitions. Lawyers now were permitted into the colony, and before long there was a flourishing bar association in the city of Savannah.

The Slave Code

One of the first acts of the assembly was to adopt a code of laws for slavery. The slave code of 1755 stated that all Negroes who were in the province and all their children should be absolute slaves. They must not be taught to read or write, and anyone who tried to teach them would be fined £15. They were to work in the fields or in the house from before daylight until after dark, but not more than sixteen hours a day. The fine for working a slave more than sixteen hours a day was £3.

If a slave left the plantation without a ticket signed by his master, he was to be whipped a maximum of twenty lashes across his bare back. No more than seven slaves could travel together unless accompanied by a white person. They could carry no firearms except by permission from their masters and then only for hunting. They could not trade for their own profit, breed horses or cattle, or keep canoes. They could not rent a room, a house, or a plantation.

Crimes punishable by death included murder, rape, poisoning a white person, and setting fire to property. A bounty would be paid for the scalp of any slave who had run away. Slaves must not be allowed to learn to be carpenters, masons, or bricklayers, since this would discourage white settlers of these trades from coming into the colony.

The code also stated that slaves should be taught the Christian religion.

Seaman Reynolds, the First Royal Governor

The first royal provincial assembly met in Savannah in January, 1755. It spent some time passing laws, but it occupied a great deal more time quarreling with Governor John Reynolds, the first royal governor. Reynolds was a seaman and had had more experience in giving orders on a ship than in handling a provincial government. He paid no attention to laws and ordered one man to be hanged two days before the appointed time. To cover his illegal acts, he altered the legislative minutes. When he could not force the assembly to do what he wanted, he dissolved it.

Reynolds brought with him William Little, a ship's surgeon, to be his private secretary. He appointed Little speaker of the assembly, and in return Little saw to it that men were elected who would obey the governor. Little became so unpopular that a grand jury ruled that he was a public nuisance.

Reynolds decided to move the capital of Georgia from Savannah to a bluff on the south side of the Ogeechee River, where he wanted to build his own town, which he called Hardwicke. He laid out a town and persuaded friends to take twenty-seven lots, but it never developed.

About the time that Georgia was made a royal province, England went to war with France. Along the Ohio and Allegheny Valley, English and French outposts claimed the same territory, and by the time Governor Reynolds arrived at Savannah, George Washington was fighting the French in western Pennsylvania. The war in America, which lasted from 1754 to 1760, was called the French and Indian War; the European and worldwide phases, 1756–1763, came to be known as the Seven Years' War.

The English government tried to raise two regiments in America and called on Georgia to do her part, but the province was so weak that the assembly replied that Georgia could not take part until the war reached its own borders. Governor Reynolds enrolled 750 men in the militia, equipped them as best he could, and ordered that they be drilled six times a year. He planned an elaborate system of forts to be built from Savannah to Frederica, up the Altamaha and Oconee rivers and across to Augusta, but Georgia was too poor to pay for the forts, and England refused to do so. Governor Reynolds constantly aggravated the people by threatening war when they could see no war near.

Along with his requests to Parliament for money for defense, Reynolds asked the Board of Trade to increase his salary. He was recalled to England in 1756 and was restored to his old post in the Navy, and he later became an admiral.

A Second Royal Governor

The king sent Henry Ellis, an explorer who had once tried to find the Northwest Passage, to be the governor of Georgia. He arrived in

Savannah in 1757. The war in the northern colonies still had not reached Georgia, but no one knew when Spain might join forces with France against England. Before coming to Georgia, Ellis secured from Parliament the promise of five hundred muskets and one small gunboat for the defense of the colony. Soon after he arrived, he inspected the southern border and recommended building some log forts. The assembly agreed, and the forts were built.

After Tomochichi's death and Oglethorpe's return to England, the Indians, who almost surrounded the colony, were not so friendly as they had been, and the settlers were nervous. When England again called on Georgia in 1757 for aid against the French in Canada, the assembly reported that the Indians could muster eight thousand warriors and that in case of Indian attacks the province was without artillery or troops and had no warships to protect the coast.

Governor Ellis met with Governor William H. Lyttleton of South Carolina and Colonel Henry Bouquet, commander of the king's forces

Sir James Wright was the third and last royal governor of Georgia. He was fair in his authority and was loved by most of the people, although he used his office to become the richest man in the colony. He believed until the end that England could hold Georgia even though the other twelve colonies were in rebellion.

George III, who ruled from 1760 to 1820, was the grandson of George II. He was greatly influenced by his domineering mother, who, it is said, always used to say to him, "Georgie, be a *king*!" He was the only king to be crowned while Georgia was a colony.

in southern America. They decided that the most important Indian chiefs should be invited to conferences in Savannah and Charles Town. The conference in Savannah in October, 1757, helped to renew and continue the friendship of the Indians.

James Wright, Third and Last Royal Governor

Because his health was not good, Governor Ellis asked for a leave of absence. Two weeks before he set sail for England, James Wright arrived to serve as lieutenant governor. Though educated in England, Wright was born in South Carolina, where he had been the attorney general for twenty years. Because of his illness, Governor Ellis never returned to Georgia, and on March 20, 1761, James Wright was made governor and commander in chief of the province of Georgia.

The same year Wright arrived in Georgia, George III succeeded to the throne of England. With great celebration he was proclaimed king in Savannah—the first and only time such an event took place on Georgia soil.

The French and Indian War finally arrived in the South and was known there as the Cherokee War. It started in 1758 and lasted until the fall of 1761, ranging from Fort Prince George in South Carolina to Fort Loudoun in eastern Tennessee. Governor Wright managed to keep friendly relations with the Creek Indians and the Cherokee War did not enter the boundaries of Georgia.

Another dangerous situation developed: Spain entered the war to help France. French privateers had raided the coast of Georgia and even entered the Savannah River. Now they were joined by Spanish raiders. The one little gunboat which Governor Ellis had provided before his departure was powerless against the enemy. Fortunately the war came to an end in 1763, and the Treaty of Paris made great changes on the Georgia border. Spain had foolishly entered the war when France was already defeated, and now England could demand what she wanted from Spain as well as France at the peace table.

England demanded Florida. France tried to save Florida for her ally, Spain, by offering England Louisiana instead. But England insisted on Florida. In exchange, she returned Cuba, which she had recently taken, to Spain.

Now the old dispute with Spain over the southern boundary of English possessions in North America was settled. Immediately, another question arose. Where did Georgia stop and Florida begin? Since Oglethorpe had maintained forts as far as the St. Johns River, it had long been accepted as the dividing line between Georgia and Florida. So the Board of Trade fixed the southern boundary of Georgia at a line drawn from the mouth of the St. Johns River west to the confluence of the Flint and Chattahoochee rivers.

The newly appointed English governor of Florida, James Grant, objected. He claimed that Florida should extend north of the St. Johns River and that the St. Marys River should be used as the boundary.

He suggested that a line be drawn from the headwaters of the St. Marys to the confluence of the Flint and the Chattahoochee rivers. Grant won the argument, and Georgia lost a large area which Oglethorpe had tried to claim for the colony.

Carolinians Move In

Now that Spain no longer held the territory between the Altamaha and St. Marys rivers, the South Carolinians claimed it. The original grant to South Carolina stated that its southern border was the St. Marys River. When the king granted Georgia to the trustees, he gave them the part of South Carolina from the Savannah River to the Altamaha River. Thus, South Carolina still claimed the land south of the Altamaha River to the St. Marys River. Carolinians filed over two hundred petitions for tracts of one thousand to two thousand acres, and Governor Thomas Boone of South Carolina deeded tracts to such prominent men as Henry Middleton and Henry Laurens, in spite of the fact that the British government had sent a circular letter to every colony saying that no one was to infringe on this land and that it belonged to the Indians.

In August, 1763, the Board of Trade sent a personal letter to Governor Boone saying that no settlements were to be made. Nevertheless, Henry Laurens cleared one hundred acres on Broughton Island and harvested his first crop there in 1767. When he loaded his boats and started them to Charles Town, however, the officials in Georgia demanded that they be cleared in Savannah, and this cost him so much that he finally gave up the project.

When the ban on slavery was lifted, Carolinians began to move across the river into Georgia, where it was less crowded. The New Englanders who had settled on a 32,000-acre tract at Midway brought fifteen hundred slaves with them and started rice and indigo plantations. At first they traded overland, going up to Savannah by the old military road, but soon they built Sunbury for a seaport. The new town grew rapidly, and in 1761 it was almost as large as Savannah and was made a port of entry.

A group of Quakers made a town on Little River just below Augusta and named their settlement Wrightsborough for Governor James Wright. A great invasion of Virginians came down through the back country and settled throughout the northwestern part of Georgia.

Everywhere the Indians were being pushed back. One means of getting land was to settle Indian debts. The Indians wanted cloth, guns, beads, and other ornaments of the white man, and having no money, they promised land in payment for these things. When the debts mounted at the trading posts, the white men demanded payment, and the Indians exchanged their land for these trifles.

As Savannah grew more populated, settlement began to spread. Putting their household belongings into a wagon, a family would gather its few cows and pigs, and off they would go. In the back country they would find a place where there was a spring and where the land looked promising. They would build a crude log cabin with a dirt floor, clear the land for planting crops, and live much like the Indians, hunting game and fish to supplement the corn and vegetables they grew.

Another family would come along and settle near them; then another. Soon the first family would move on to new territory, and more and more newcomers would arrive to fill the settlement. A village would grow up. A merchant would act as the factor or broker for the farmers, helping them to sell their products. The settlers would build a church, and a preacher would come to save their souls and a doctor to take care of their ills.

Rice and Riches

Along the marshy regions of the coast, rice now grew on land that had been worthless without slaves. The planter chose a location far enough up a creek so the salt water would not kill the rice plants. At the same time, the tide must flood and drain the fields. Land along the rivers and creeks for about ten miles could be used, and rice plantations soon were located on every usable stream.

The canals that supplied water for flooding and draining the fields were dug by slaves using shovel and wheelbarrow, and the excavated earth was piled up to heighten the banks. The banks were used as roads and the canals as waterways for the flat boats which took the rice to the threshing barns.

The trunk, or floodgate, was a wooden culvert through the banks with a wooden door at either end. Seed was planted at the time of the new moon and the full moon, to take advantage of the high tides flooding the fields as soon as the planting was completed. Then the trunks were closed for from three to six days, to encourage sprouting, to keep birds from eating the seed, and to kill grass. When the trunks were opened and the fields drained, the young rice could be cultivated. The next flooding stayed on the crop for about two weeks, followed by forty days of dry cultivation. After that, the harvest flow remained on the crop until it was ripe.

Sometime between August and October, when the fields were ready for harvest, the field was drained, and the slaves went in to cut the rice. The men rolled up their trouser legs above the knees and the women tied strings around their waists and pulled their skirts up over them, making a kind of bustle around the hips.

In the left hand they grasped a handful of rice stalks, and using the rice hook with the right hand, they cut the stalks about a foot above the ground. They left the stalks lying on the rice stubble to dry and later tied them into sheaves and carried them to the plantation mill to be threshed.

To thresh the grain, the rice was spread on a sheet and beaten with a double-jointed flail. An ordinary flail, used for wheat or oats, consisted of a handle and a hinged swiple or swingle, with which the grain is pounded, to separate the kernels from the straw. A rice flail, however, carried two hinged swiples, which made a flapping motion as they were

102

worked, tossing up the light straw so that the wind—called Tony by the Negroes—could whisk it away.

The grain and what straw remained were scooped up into a large round, shallow, basket-woven tray with a slanting rim, known as a fanner. The rice was bounced up and down, or fanned, to finish separating the straw from the grain. Again, Tony was called on to help blow away the straw.

Each grain of rice is enclosed in a tough fibrous husk, and to remove this the early Georgians used a mortar made from a cypress log and a pestle about three feet long. Rice grains were put into the mortar and pounded with the pestle. After husking, the rice grains were poured into large barrels called tierces, each of which would hold seven hundred pounds of rice.

Raising rice provided employment for slaves the year around. Planting, cultivating, and harvesting went on in the spring, summer, and fall. Threshing was done in the winter, and as soon as it was finished, ditches had to be cleaned and banks repaired.

Rice was a profitable crop to raise if a man owned enough slaves, and like the plantation owners in South Carolina, the rice planters in Georgia quickly grew wealthy. They soon built fine plantation houses and owned hundreds of slaves.

Darien, a Lumber Port

Up the Altamaha River in the interior of Georgia, great trees of long-leaf yellow pine were cut and floated down the river to Darien. Far up the river where the trees were cut, a raft was made of fifty to seventy-five logs. Two logs were fastened in a V-shaped bow; other logs were wedged tightly into it and held in place by cross binders laid on top of the logs. A long sweep shaped like the blade of an oar was mounted at the bow and stern to steer the raft.

A crew of three men lived on the raft for the three or four days it took to float it down the river. Cooking was done on planks covered with sand, and sometimes a small tent was provided for shelter.

The logs were stored in pens called booms, which lined the river edges for miles near Darien. As they were needed, they were hauled to the mills where they were cut into lumber. Then they were carried all over the world in the wooden sailing ships which crowded the wharves.

The raft hands lived a rough life. Summer and winter they lived in the open. Around the streets of Darien a raft hand was known by the tin coffee pot and iron skillet fastened to his belt on one side, an ax hanging from the other, and a great coil of manila rope thrown over one shoulder. They mingled with sailors from foreign ships, who made music on their Jew's harps and accordions and sang songs in strange languages.

Georgia exported many raw products from her fields and forests. During the 1760's and 1770's, ships carried out of the port of Savannah silk, timber, shingles, hoops, spars, pitch, turpentine, cord wood, lime, indigo, rice, corn, oranges, orange juice, ground nuts, tallow, myrtle, honey, reeds, horses, oxen, cattle, hogs and hog products, geese, chickens, turkeys, deerskins, raccoon skins, beaver skins, otter skins, cow hides, cow horns, sturgeon, leather, lumber, staves, handspikes, oars, tar, cedar posts, pink root, sago powder, cotton, peas, potatoes, candles, and beeswax.

Trade to the West Indies brought Georgians a little gold and silver, but exports sent to England were paid for with manufactured goods instead of money, because England did not want the colonies to have cash, which would enable them to buy products from other countries. Under the trustees they had local paper money called sola bills, but when Georgia became a royal colony, Parliament passed a law forbidding any colony to issue its own paper currency. It seemed that Georgia would have to struggle along with a few stray Spanish coins.

There was no printing press or newspaper in Georgia for its first thirty years, and books and pamphlets were published in Charles Town until 1762, when James Johnston set up a shop in Savannah. He began by publishing the official papers of the assembly and in 1763 started publication of the first newspaper in the colony, the *Georgia Gazette*.

Englishmen or Americans?

Savannah remained the social and intellectual center of the province. Wealthy Georgians had town houses as well as plantations bearing such names as Hermitage, Valambrossa, Hope, Silk Hope, Isle of Hope, Wormsloe, Cedar Grove, Laurel Hill, Orange Grove, Mulberry Hill, Wild Horn, and Lee Hall. In going back and forth they used their carriages, phaetons, and riding chairs. The richest man in Georgia was Governor James Wright, and John Graham was said to be the second wealthiest. Graham had an English gardener and twenty-three house servants.

Men and women dressed in the finest clothes and jewelry to be had from England: silk mitts, wigs, white kid gloves, satin bonnets, painted hose, silk breeches, gold necklaces, silver earrings, gold rings set with amethysts and diamonds, and gold and silver breastpins. Those who feared thunderstorms protected their houses with lightning conductors.

There were others in Georgia, however, who did not have these luxuries. The middle-class people were respectable and hard-working but not wealthy. Poor people found it as hard to get along in Georgia as in England. At the bottom of the social and economic structure were the Negro slaves.

Horses were as valuable property as slaves, and horse stealing was profitable business. For this crime some were hanged, some were pardoned, and some made their escape, as did William Saxe, who was said to have broken out of jail twenty-eight times.

Georgia adopted the Church of England as the provincial religion in 1758. The province was divided into eight parishes, and a tax was levied to pay the salaries of the clergymen. Membership in the Church of England was not compulsory. A Georgian could be Lutheran, Congregationalist, Presbyterian, Baptist, or Jew, but everyone had to pay taxes for the upkeep of the Church of England.

Gradually, Georgians came to be much like the members of the other English colonies. Although the weakest and youngest of the colonies, Georgia developed rapidly, and by the time of the Revolution her citizens were living, building, and trading like those in Carolina, which was more than sixty years older.

The colony of Georgia was only forty-three years old when the Revolution started. Most of the people living there had either come from England or were first-generation Americans who had had little intercourse with older Americans either by travel or trade. They were still Englishmen rather than Americans.

CHAPTER EIGHT

A Question of Loyalty

The French and Indian War in America enlarged the dominions of England, but it also doubled her national debt. The king thought that the American colonies should be taxed to raise additional revenue. Taxpayers in England were already paying heavily, and it seemed only fair that Americans be taxed, because a large part of the nation's war debt had been contracted in defending the colonies from the French and Spanish.

The colonists saw matters differently. They claimed that, by furnishing soldiers for the French and Indian War and helping the English defeat the French in Canada, they had already paid their part. In addition, for England to tax the colonists was unjust, according to the English Bill of Rights. The colonies were not represented in Parliament, and taxation without representation was illegal. As Americans, the colonists believed the tax to be unfair, and as Englishmen they believed it to infringe on their rights.

A Reluctant Decision

As the youngest of the colonies, Georgia was the least upset by the idea of English taxation. She was the pet of Parliament, which had provided more than a million dollars for her support. Gratitude might well have made Georgia the last stronghold of English loyalty in America.

In the spring of 1765 Parliament passed a Stamp Act. All paper used for marriage certificates, deeds, records, contracts, notes, bonds, or any legal purposes had to be stamped, and the stamp had to be paid for. Tracts, pamphlets, and newspapers could not be sold unless printed on stamped paper. Cargo manifests had to carry stamps, and so did university degrees. It was a tax that hit everyone.

Sometimes the stamp was embossed directly on the paper. More generally the stamps were printed on coarse blue paper known as tobacco paper and were cut apart and placed on the document. To secure the stamp, a small strip of tinfoil was attached to the stamp. The ends of the tinfoil were passed through a cut in the parchment or paper to which the stamp was attached. The ends were flattened on the opposite side and a smaller stamp engraved with the crown and cipher of the king was pasted over the foil to secure it.

Most Georgians felt that the tax was as fair as any that could be put upon them, and although a few Georgians questioned England's right to levy the tax, the majority were willing to submit. But it was too much for James Johnston, the printer, to pay. In December, 1765, he was forced to discontinue publishing the *Georgia Gazette*.

News of the stamp law reached America long before the stamps were printed and sent over. Because it was so universal a tax, it brought out universal condemnation. Everybody hated it. Indignation grew, and rebel leaders in the northern colonies called a Stamp Act Congress to meet in New York. Georgia was invited to send a representative, but when the assembly met in September to appoint a delegate, Governor Wright persuaded them not to send one. They did, however, send an observer to bring back a report on what the congress did.

South Carolinians were incensed that the Georgians were so apathetic, and some of the other colonies also called the Georgians unpatriotic because they had not sent a delegate to the Stamp Act Congress.

A Few Rebels

Some Savannah businessmen soon found the tax expensive, and gradually they began to organize opposition in Savannah. In the back country, where settlers from other colonies were accustomed to thinking of themselves more as Americans than as Georgians, opposition grew more rapidly. Soon the organized groups took the name of Sons of Liberty, or Liberty Boys, which was already used in the twelve colonies to the north.

November 1, 1765, was the time set for the Stamp Act to go into effect, but it was not until December 5 that His Majesty's sloop *Speedwell* arrived at Savannah with supplies of stamps and stamped paper on board. Because of rumors that a band of Liberty Boys intended to seize the stamps and paper, a guard of forty men protected the dockhands while they unloaded it and put it into the king's store, where it remained until January 3, 1766, when the king's agent arrived at Savannah to begin distribution. He landed secretly in a scout boat with an officer and party of men to guard him and hurried to the governor's house, where he took the oath of office. The Liberty Boys in Savannah had become so strong that the agent remained a prisoner for two weeks, not daring to show himself on the streets.

Governor Wright received threatening letters, and James Habersham, president of the king's council, was attacked one night and sought protection in the governor's house, which was guarded. Toward the end of January, Governor Wright learned that six hundred Liberty Boys planned to break into the king's store, so he moved the paper to Fort George on Cockspur Island. On February 2, the *Speedwell* returned to Savannah, and the paper was put on board, but the sight of the ship set off trouble. An effigy of Governor Wright holding one of the obnoxious stamped sheets in his hand was carried through the streets and burned.

This show of patriotism still did not satisfy the South Carolinians. They were angry because the Georgians had allowed a few captains to clear their cargoes using stamped ship's papers. They threatened to burn any Georgia ship coming into Charles Town Harbor and to put to death any South Carolinian who traded with a Georgian.

Although Governor Wright had talked the assembly out of sending a delegate to the Stamp Act Congress, he now faced stronger opposition. Late in January, 1766, he was ordered by the English government to requisition the assembly for supplies for the English soldiers stationed in Georgia. The upper house agreed, but the lower house voted against the requisition.

To further complicate matters, the lower house refused to approve any agent to represent the colony in England which the upper house nominated. So Georgia was without an agent in England until 1768, when Benjamin Franklin, the agent for Pennsylvania, agreed to act for Georgia also. He did such a good job that he became a hero to the colony, which he never visited, and when Georgia became a state, a county was named for him.

Governor Wright was indignant at the action of the assembly, but he was powerless. If he dissolved the assembly, the Sons of Liberty might be able to control a larger majority in a new one. The government of Georgia was at a standstill.

Noble Wymberley Jones was an ardent Liberty Boy, even though his father, who had come over with Oglethorpe, was a Loyalist. Had it not been for his father's illness, Noble Wymberley Jones would have been one of the signers of the Declaration of Independence.

110

Three weeks later the Stamp Act was repealed by Parliament, whose members had been astonished by the bitter opposition the measure had aroused. Still, the protest was only postponed. The next year Parliament passed the Townshend Act, by which it taxed all glass, lead, paper, and tea imported into the colonies.

The Patriots Organize

In 1769 a protest meeting was held. The Georgia Liberty Boys agreed to follow the lead of the other colonies. They resolved to manufacture their own products and to buy no English goods except necessities. They would buy no slaves from England, and they would not do business with anyone in Georgia who opposed this agreement.

Jonathan Bryan presided over the meeting. He had been a boy in Pocataligo, South Carolina, when his father, Joseph Bryan, had come with William Bull to help Oglethorpe choose a site for the colony. Jonathan came to Georgia in 1750, petitioned for a grant of five hundred acres, and established Walnut Hill Plantation. In 1769 he was a member of the king's council, but he was an ardent Son of Liberty and openly protested the English taxes. When orders came from London commanding his suspension from the council, he rose and said that it was not necessary to expel him, that he would resign at once.

Governor Wright upheld the royal authority, but although he was well liked, he could not prevent opposition in the assembly. Noble Wymberley Jones, Patriot son of Noble Jones, Loyalist, was elected speaker of the assembly. When the assembly agreed to the Patriots' resolution, however, Governor Wright dissolved the legislature.

In 1771 Governor Wright went to England on a leave of absence. The king appointed James Habersham president of the council. Habersham agreed with the Patriots in theory, but he remained a Loyalist as long as he held the office.

Twice the house elected Noble W. Jones as speaker, and each time

Peter Tondee, who came to Savannah from Switzerland as a small boy, at the death of his parents became one of the first children to live at the Bethesda Orphanage. Later, his tavern was the meeting place for the Liberty Boys, and the Declaration of Independence was first read in Georgia at Tondee's Tavern.

Habersham vetoed the election. The third time, Jones declined, and Archibald Bulloch, another Patriot, was elected.

Governor Wright returned in the spring of 1773. He left at once for Augusta, where, for payment of $200,000 worth of debts due English and Scots traders, he gained from the Indians some two million acres of land, from which the original Wilkes County was formed in 1777. Like Wilkes-Barre, Pennsylvania, and John Wilkes Booth, it was named for the English political reformer Wilkes, a stout supporter in Parliament of the colonists' cause.

Finding the colonies stubborn, Parliament repealed the tax on everything except tea. The Americans were not pacified, however, and they resolved to outlaw the taxed commodity. Tea brought to New York and Philadelphia was refused, and the ships were sent back to England. In Charles Town chests of tea were taken ashore but were stored in damp cellars and left to rot. In Boston a group of Liberty Boys disguised as Indians dumped the tea into the harbor in the famous Boston Tea Party. All of these actions helped to keep alive the flame of the Patriots in Georgia.

Tondee's Tavern, Liberty's Headquarters

Up to this time, the organization of the Patriots in Savannah had been centered in the assembly, but now Tondee's Tavern became the meeting place for the men who were to make the decisions. Peter Tondee had come to Savannah from Switzerland when he was a boy, but the death of his mother and father made him one of the first children to live in the Bethesda Orphanage. In fact, Peter helped to build the orphanage, and by 1750 he was one of three young men who formed the Union Society to help provide financial help for the orphanage.

In time, Peter bought land, and in 1766 he built Tondee's Tavern on what is now the corner of Broughton and Whitaker Streets in Savannah. It was a family tavern, and while the parents drank their ale, the young people played quoits. Some of the young men formed a weekly club called the All Saints Club.

The Quoits Club became more political as the disagreement with England grew stronger, and on July 27, 1774, when the news arrived from Boston that English troops had closed the port there, many speeches were made at Tondee's Tavern. Archibald Bulloch, John Houston, George Walton, and Noble Wymberley Jones, the four

George Walton, signer of the Declaration of Independence.

113

Patriot leaders, decided to take no action yet but to call another meeting on August 10.

Governor Wright heard about the plot and forbade the meeting, so it was held in great secrecy. Peter Tondee stood at the door and checked every man who entered to make sure of his loyalty. At the meeting they passed a resolution of grievances and voted to send six hundred barrels of rice and as much cash as they could raise to Boston.

Among the most patriotic members of this meeting were the Massachusetts men from Midway. These people could still remember the religious quarrel which had led to their settlement in New England. Lyman Hall, one of the Midway representatives, demanded a complete break with England, but the Georgia Sons of Liberty were not yet ready to go that far.

On August 10, 1774, Governor Wright called a meeting of loyal citizens to try to check the spreading hostility toward England. Many of the older colonists did not want to take radical action, but a resolution was voted to discourage any future meetings of the Sons of Liberty.

Among the more than sixty Loyalists were James Habersham, father of Patriots James and Joseph Habersham, and Noble Jones, father of Patriot Noble Wymberley Jones. From St. George's Parish in what is now Jefferson County came another protest against the Sons of Liberty, signed by seventy-five men who lived on the frontier and were afraid of Indian attacks if the English soldiers were withdrawn from the forts. They blamed the whole affair on the meddlesome people from New England.

The Massachusetts men were not able to persuade the Patriots to join the Nonimportation Association approved by the First Continental Congress, to which Georgia had not sent a representative. The Midway colonists went to South Carolina and asked to work with that colony, but South Carolina would have nothing to do with its conservative neighbor. The Carolina Patriots not only turned down the request

The Sons of Liberty break open the powder magazine.

of the transplanted Puritans but also threatened to invade Georgia and annex it to South Carolina.

The Georgians Still Wait

The Georgians who met at Tondee's Tavern in January, 1775, as the First Provincial Congress, were still hopeful that England would listen to America's demands. They sent a plea to the king to repeal the acts passed by Parliament in which the colonies were not represented. The king, however, could not legally repeal an Act of Parliament, and he also needed the money from the taxes.

When the news of the Battle of Lexington arrived in Savannah on May 10, 1775, it set off a celebration. Led by Noble W. Jones, Edward Telfair, Joseph Habersham, and John Milledge, the Patriots raided the powder magazine, property of the king. They sent part of the powder with another shipment of rice and some money to Boston. Governor Wright offered a reward of £150 for the arrest of the leaders, but no arrests followed because of public sympathy for the rioters.

When the Provincial Congress was called to meet again in Savannah on July 5, 1775, the Quakers stated that they did not approve of fighting, but the following year, when war was declared, they proved that they could fight as well as the New Englanders. This time an effort was made to send representatives to the Continental Congress, and three were chosen: Noble W. Jones, Archibald Bulloch, and John Houstoun. Since only five of the twelve parishes were represented, however, the delegates did not go to Philadelphia but sent a letter to John Hancock, the president of the Continental Congress.

The Midway people held a separate meeting at which Dr. Lyman Hall was elected to represent their parish at the Continental Congress. Dr. Hall went to Philadelphia and sat in the session, but since he represented only one parish, he was not allowed to vote.

The American Revolution caused cruel disruptions in the lives of Georgians. Families were divided, father against son, brother against brother. Many Loyalists tried to be neutral and moved their families to Florida to wait until the war was over.

The old men who had been born in England and who had come to Georgia in the service of their king could not refute their loyalty to him. The younger men who had no sentiment about England and whose minds looked forward rather than backward were eager to separate from England and go their own way. Both Patriots and Loyalists hoped to avert war, but eventually each man was forced to choose his side.

CHAPTER NINE

The Showdown

The Reverend John J. Zubly was the pastor of the Independent Presbyterian Church of Savannah. He came from Switzerland and was such a good preacher that sometimes the Anglican church was deserted on Sundays, all of its congregation going to hear Mr. Zubly's sermons against England.

Not only did he protest from the pulpit; he wrote pamphlets and articles denouncing the British government. The Patriots counted him as one of their strongest members.

The Minister Changes His Mind

By the time the king's birthday arrived on June 4, 1775, everyone in Georgia knew that the Patriots and Loyalists would soon clash. As usual, Governor Wright prepared to celebrate the king's birthday by placing cannon on the river bluff to be fired, but someone spiked the cannon and rolled them down the bank.

On June 5, the Liberty Boys erected a liberty pole in front of Tondee's Tavern and celebrated. Two weeks later they elected a Council of Safety to correspond with the other colonies. The revolutionaries raised their new flag to the top of the liberty pole, ate a dinner that Peter Tondee provided, and drank a toast to each of the thirteen colonies.

More than a hundred delegates from all parts of the colony attended the Second Provincial Congress at Tondee's Tavern on July 4, 1775,

117

The Liberty Boys raise a liberty pole in front of Tondee's Tavern. Georgia's new flag was flown from the top of the pole.

just one year before the Declaration of Independence was signed. Archibald Bulloch was elected president and George Walton secretary. Before beginning their business, the members went to church, where Pastor Zubly preached a sermon on the alarming state of affairs in the colonies.

Back at Tondee's Tavern the congress drew up another set of resolutions, blaming Parliament for their grievances. They sent another petition to the king asking him to change the laws Parliament had made against the colonies.

They announced to the people of Georgia that a civil war had begun in America and informed Governor Wright of what they had done and why. They said that the people had set up the Provincial Congress because he had dissolved the assembly.

Wright was helpless. He had tried in May to reconvene the royal assembly, but the members refused. His power was gone.

The Provincial Congress took over the courts and militia. Governor

Wright asked Parliament to send troops to help him enforce the law, but by then the British army was besieged in Boston and fully occupied. Wright then asked to be recalled, but he was instructed to stay in Georgia and try to keep order in the colony.

Zubly was a natural representative to the Continental Congress in Philadelphia, and in 1775 he was elected along with Noble W. Jones, Archibald Bulloch, Lyman Hall, and John Houstoun to represent Georgia. In Philadelphia, however, Zubly began to weaken. Although he had preached against taxation without representation, he had not advocated separation from England. When he realized that the Continental Congress wanted immediate separation, he found that he was more Loyalist than Patriot.

Upset by the radical steps being taken by the congress, Zubly tried to get in touch with Governor Wright. When this was discovered and he was confronted with it on the floor of the congress, Zubly resigned and

This portrait of Archibald Bulloch and his family was painted by Henry Benbridge, a Philadelphia artist who moved to Charles Town, South Carolina. Bulloch was president of two Provincial Congresses and was the first president of the first republican government organized on Georgia soil.

returned to Georgia. He continued to preach and to publish pamphlets, but now they were against the Patriots' cause.

A Skirmish over Rice

In January, 1776, three English war vessels anchored off Tybee to obtain supplies. An attack was expected at any moment, and to prevent Governor Wright's ordering them to be used against the colony, the Council of Safety ordered his arrest. Joseph Habersham and several other men entered the governor's mansion, where Wright was meeting with his council. They arrested the governor, and the councilmen fled.

Governor Wright gave Habersham his word of honor not to communicate with the war vessels, and the Patriots let him remain in the mansion. On the night of February 11, however, Wright slipped out of his house and went to Bonaventure Plantation, where his friend, John Mullryne, lived. A boat was waiting and took him through Tybee Creek to the English ship *Scarborough*. He went aboard at three o'clock on the morning of February 12. Most Georgians were glad that he got away, for he had been a good governor and a friend to many of them.

The Patriots began to prepare Savannah for an attack, building fortifications along the waterfront. Having waited off Tybee over a month without supplies, the English in the warships decided to take a fleet of rice boats. They sailed up the river toward the wharves, and before the Georgians could stop them, they had seized the rice boats.

Savannah leaders tried to recover the boats by negotiation, but the English refused to release them. Outraged, the Georgians asked for help from South Carolina. When a group of Carolina militia arrived, they boarded some of the boats and set fire to them. The English left with only a few of the prizes. This was the first activity against the mother country by Georgia.

Another Provincial Congress was held, but the members did not go to hear Pastor Zubly preach as they had before. Archibald Bulloch, Button

Gwinnett, Lyman Hall, George Walton, and John Houstoun were elected to go to the Continental Congress in Philadelphia that summer, but Bulloch could not go because of business.

Button Gwinnett, an Englishman by birth, had lived in Georgia only a few years, but he was an ardent Patriot. George Walton was from an old Virginia family, and Lyman Hall was a physician who had moved to Midway from Connecticut.

Soon after the Georgia representatives reached Philadelphia, they heard that John Zubly was converting Patriots into Loyalists. John Houstoun went back to Savannah to try to stop the minister, and for this reason he was not in Philadelphia when the Declaration of Independence was signed.

As for John Zubly, he was banished from Savannah in 1777 and went to South Carolina. When Savannah fell to the English in 1778, he returned, but his health failed rapidly, and he died in 1781, on the eve of the evacuation of the city by the English.

With Liberty and Justice for All

On August 10, 1776, Tondee's Tavern was the scene of the most memorable event of its history. There the Declaration of Independence was read to the Council of Safety by President Archibald Bulloch, with the names of Button Gwinnett, George Walton, and Lyman Hall appended as representatives of Georgia.

After reading it to the Council of Safety, President Bulloch went outside and read the Declaration in the public square, where throngs of people had gathered. The people demanded that it be read again, and this time Bulloch read it before the liberty pole in front of Tondee's Tavern. Later in the afternoon the famous document was read for the fourth time at the spot where Oglethorpe had landed. Up and down the bluffs of the Savannah River the noise of cannon echoed in a salute of thirteen guns.

Everyone in Savannah stopped work and proclaimed a holiday. In

Button Gwinnett, George Walton, and Lyman Hall, the three Georgians who signed the Declaration of Independence. In later years, both Gwinnett and Hall served as governor of the state and Walton was chief magistrate of the commonwealth.

the streets and in the taverns, which did a roaring business, the Declaration was discussed. Messengers were sent to the back country, and the celebration went on, settlement by settlement, as the word spread. In Savannah some of the Patriots made a mock funeral cortege with the effigy of King George III in the coffin. So far as they were concerned, King George was dead.

There was one person missing in this celebration who deserved to see it. Peter Tondee had died nearly a year before, on October 22, 1775. His wife now ran the tavern.

The State of Georgia

One of the first acts of President Bulloch and the Provincial Congress was to begin the organization of the State of Georgia. The name "Provincial Congress" was changed to "Assembly," and a committee was elected to write a state constitution. Work on the constitution was begun in October, 1776, and was completed on February 5, 1777.

The new constitution contained sixty-three articles and provided for executive, legislative, and judiciary branches. In order to vote, a man had to be a Protestant, twenty-one years old, and white, and had to own 250 acres of land and have lived in the state at least twelve months.

Schools were to be erected in each county and supported by the state. Everyone was guaranteed freedom of religion, freedom of the press, and trial by jury.

Now that Georgia was committed to the Revolution, South Carolina was friendly again. When an English ship loaded with powder appeared off the coast, the Provincial Congress placed Oliver Bowen and Joseph Habersham in charge of a boat to help the South Carolinians. Georgians and Carolinians captured the ship and took nine thousand pounds of powder, five thousand pounds of which they sent to the Continental Congress.

Fortunately, not until after the battles of Trenton, Princeton, Brandywine, Germantown, Saratoga, and Monmouth did the English turn their attention to the South. There now began a bitter civil war in the new State of Georgia.

The Realities of Independence

The Patriots did not wait for the English to attack. They began military activities immediately, and Loyalists, together with runaway slaves and hostile Indians, flocked to Florida, where they organized the Florida Rangers. The Rangers made guerrilla attacks on south Georgia settlements, and Captain John Baker, with seventy mounted volunteers from St. John's Parish, marched to the St. Marys River to surprise a fort which the Rangers held. An English ship supported the fort, however, and Baker was forced to retreat.

The Continental Congress in Philadelphia recommended that Georgia, South Carolina, and North Carolina take St. Augustine. Jonathan Bryan, John Houstoun, and Lachlan McIntosh went to Charles Town to confer with General Charles Lee, commander of the Continental troops in the South. They agreed that St. Augustine should be attacked immediately. The Continental Congress appropriated $60,000 for two additional battalions of Continental troops, four ships, and two forts to be built at Savannah and Sunbury.

General Lee sent Generals Robert Howe and William Moultrie with their troops to Savannah. They marched off to Florida, but got no farther south than Sunbury because of lack of equipment, poor administration, and the hot weather. They returned to Charles Town in less than a month, without having seen the enemy, and Georgia was left defenseless.

Troops in Georgia consisted of a battalion of 236 men under the command of Colonel Lachlan McIntosh, a few cavalry, sixty men along the Florida border, and a few scattered troops on the frontiers for protection against the Indians.

A Duel Brings Death

After signing the Declaration of Independence, Button Gwinnett came home from Philadelphia with instructions from the Continental Congress for raising an army in Georgia. As he rode the eight hundred miles on horseback, Gwinnett saw himself as a military commander.

Button Gwinnett, signer of the Declaration of Independence. His signature, because of its rarity, is now one of the most valuable in the world.

When he arrived in Savannah, however, he learned that Colonel McIntosh, who was a good friend of George Walton, had been appointed general of the Continental forces in Georgia.

The McIntoshes had come to Georgia as poor refugees, but now they were wealthy and had large plantations near Darien. Lachlan and his brother William had fought with Oglethorpe at Bloody Marsh against the Spaniards when they were youngsters. Lachlan McIntosh felt that he deserved the rank of general and accepted his responsibilities seriously.

Early in 1777, President Archibald Bulloch died, and Button Gwinnett was made acting president until a regular election could be held. Gwinnett saw a chance to be more important than Lachlan McIntosh. He not only would capture St. Augustine but also would conquer all of Florida and annex it to Georgia.

As president of the state, he assumed complete command of all forces in Georgia. When he appointed a military council, with himself as president, to control militia and Continental military officers, General McIntosh refused to accept Gwinnett's authority and ignored the council.

Colonel Samuel Elbert was in charge of the expedition to take Florida. Sawpit Bluff on the St. Johns River was to be the rendezvous. John Baker, now a colonel, with the Georgia militia went by land, and the Continental troops under Colonel Elbert went by boat. When the two forces did not arrive at the same time, each had to fight the enemy alone. By the end of May the expedition was a complete failure, and the troops returned to Savannah. Gwinnett was blamed not only as commander in chief but also as president.

While still acting president, Gwinnett had received a letter from John Hancock, president of the Continental Congress at Philadelphia, accusing George McIntosh, another brother of Lachlan, of treason. Hancock said he had learned that George McIntosh was helping William Panton buy rice for the British forces in Florida. George McIntosh was a member of the Georgia Assembly, and the charge was serious.

John Adam Treutlen, Georgia's first governor. He was a Salzburger, and even though many of his countrymen remained loyal to the English, Treutlen was a staunch Patriot.

When Hancock's letter reached Gwinnett, the Assembly had already adjourned. The acting president took the responsibility of ordering the arrest of George McIntosh, as Hancock had instructed. McIntosh was brought to Savannah and turned over to the provost marshal, who put him in irons.

McIntosh's friends proposed bail of £50,000, but Gwinnett refused. A few days later, when Gwinnett went to Sunbury, the Assembly released George McIntosh on £2,000 bail.

On May 1, when the Assembly met to elect a successor to President Bulloch, it ignored Gwinnett and elected John Adam Treutlen. Two weeks later, on May 15, both Gwinnett and Lachlan McIntosh were called before the Assembly to account for the failure in Florida. Gwinnett spoke so well for himself that the Assembly approved his conduct and released him from any blame.

McIntosh was enraged. He lost his temper and called Gwinnett a scoundrel and a lying rascal. Though this was a breach of the rules, the

Assembly made no comment on McIntosh's rudeness. Gwinnett, however, considered it an affair of honor. His friends agreed that he would have to challenge McIntosh to a duel.

As his second, Gwinnett selected George Wells, a member of the Assembly from near Augusta. Wells presented General McIntosh with a letter from Gwinnett saying that because McIntosh had called him a scoundrel, he desired to satisfy his honor in a duel with McIntosh the next morning before sunrise. McIntosh accepted, although he said it was earlier than his usual time of rising. He chose Major James Habersham as his second. They agreed to use pistols and to meet in the Sir James Wright meadow near Thunderbolt.

Next morning the pistols were examined to be sure that each held only one charge. The two men stood face to face, forty paces apart. At the signal, two shots sounded simultaneously. Gwinnett fell. McIntosh's bullet had struck him in the leg above the knee and broken

When Button Gwinnett challenged Lachlan McIntosh to a duel, each man's bullet slightly wounded the other. McIntosh recovered promptly, but Gwinnett's wound mortified, and he died three days later.

the bone. Gwinnett had hit McIntosh in the muscular part of the leg. McIntosh limped over to Gwinnett, and the two men shook hands.

By modern standards, neither wound was serious, but the weather was hot, and Gwinnett's wound turned gangrenous. Three days later he died.

Gwinnett's friends presented to Governor Treutlen a petition with five hundred names on it demanding that General McIntosh leave Georgia. Gwinnett's wife declared publicly that McIntosh was not to blame for the death of her husband, but George Walton arranged a transfer for General McIntosh. He was sent to serve under Washington at Valley Forge.

Because he was a signer of the Declaration of Independence, Button Gwinnett lives in history, but his chief claim to fame is the rareness of his signature, now a collector's item. Only thirty-six copies are known to exist and one has sold for as much as $50,000.

As for George McIntosh, Governor Treutlen had him arrested and sent to Philadelphia to be tried for treason by the Continental Congress. George escaped and made his way to the McIntosh plantation on the Georgia coast, where he hid in the swamp. Friends finally persuaded him to go back to Philadelphia and stand trial. He was freed because of insufficient evidence and returned to Georgia, where he continued to fight for the Patriots.

Rumors Confirmed

Colonel Samuel Elbert took over the Continental Army in Georgia. Most men, however, preferred to enlist in the Georgia militia and remain near home rather than join the Continental Army, where the discipline was stricter and they might be sent north at any time.

The Florida Rangers had been reinforced by a band of five or six hundred Loyalists called Scopholites, so called because they were led by a colonel named Scovel, or Scophol. The Rangers had raided the banks of the Altamaha River and sent spies as far as Savannah.

Colonel Samuel Elbert, leader of the Continental Army in Georgia.

Trying to invade Florida had become a habit for the Georgians, and in 1778 they prepared for their second annual attempt. The Assembly promised a roving commission to anyone who would raise fifteen fighting men. The commission entitled him to plunder and loot in Florida and to keep whatever he took.

On January 10, 1778, the Assembly elected John Houstoun governor of Georgia. He decided to command the Georgia militia himself, but there were only 350 men. Colonel Elbert had about 500 Georgia Continentals. General Robert Howe, who had replaced General Lee as commander of the Southern Department, led the Continental regulars from South Carolina to Savannah. All the forces were to meet at Fort Howe on the Altamaha River.

Elbert reached Fort Howe in April, and while waiting for the other troops, he sent a force down the Altamaha and captured three English ships near Frederica. July came, but still the forces were scattered from

Savannah to the St. Marys River. Houstoun refused to take orders from Howe, and Howe refused to obey Houstoun.

Finally, Howe gave up the expedition. On July 5, 1778, encamped at the abandoned English Fort Tonyn on the St. Marys River, he wrote that the expedition had failed because of jealousy between Continental troops and militia, lack of preparations, swampy country, and the hot climate.

For three years troops had marched up and down the coast of Georgia to no avail. By the middle of November, 1778, rumors reached Georgia that England had decided to attack her from the sea, from the north, and from Florida.

The Florida forces had already set out. Lieutenant Colonel Mark Prevost commanded one hundred English regulars with three hundred Indians and Scopholites. Lieutenant Colonel L. V. Fuser brought five hundred men by water. These two forces were to meet at Midway and march on Savannah, where Colonel Archibald Campbell, who was sailing from New York with two thousand regulars, would attack from the sea.

The English planned to rectify the failure of Saratoga by conquering Georgia and beginning a triumphant march to the north.

CHAPTER TEN

The Bitter Struggle

Robert Howe of North Carolina was one of the earliest and most ardent Patriots. When the Revolution began, he was made colonel of the First North Carolina Regiment, and in December, 1775, he fought at Norfolk, Virginia, against Lord Dunmore. On February 29, 1776, the Continental Congress appointed him brigadier general; after fighting in Virginia in 1778, Howe was placed in command of the southern army. After the unsuccessful attack on St. Augustine in the summer of 1778, General Howe led his troops back to Sunbury, where he stayed until November, at which time the rumors reached Georgia that the British planned to attack the southernmost state.

General Augustine Prevost sent his brother, Lieutenant Colonel Mark Prevost, to command the English troops on land. He was joined by Colonel Daniel McGirth, a Loyalist who had defected from the American side and joined the Rangers.

Daniel McGirth was a South Carolinian who first joined the Patriot side as a scout. He was an ignorant man but an expert woodsman and a dead shot, and he came to Georgia riding a horse named Grey Goose. An American officer saw the horse and wanted to buy it, but McGirth said that Grey Goose was more important to him than money.

The officer began to harass McGirth, and finally the scout struck his superior and swore at him. McGirth was court-martialed, imprisoned, and whipped. When he saw Grey Goose tied to a tree outside the prison,

Daniel McGirth's escape.

McGirth broke down the bars of the window and escaped, jumping on his horse and dashing away.

He joined the Florida Rangers and was made a colonel in the English army. When the war was over, he returned to South Carolina and lived quietly with his wife.

The English troops reached the Altamaha River about the middle of November and two weeks later marched to Midway. Colonel John Baker hastily gathered a few Georgia militia to try to stop Prevost. They met where the Savannah and Darien road crossed Bulltown swamp, but after a short skirmish the Americans were forced to retreat.

Come and Take It

Colonel John White, with about one hundred Continentals and militia and two pieces of artillery, built a breastwork across the road near the

Midway meetinghouse. White hoped to stop Prevost long enough for reinforcements to arrive from Savannah.

Before Prevost appeared, Colonel White was joined by General James Screven with twenty militiamen. They abandoned the site at the church and set out to make an ambush about a mile and a half south of Midway, where the road was bordered by a thick wood. McGirth knew this part of the country also, and he suggested to Prevost that they plan an ambush at the same place. The enemies arrived almost simultaneously, and without either being able to set up an ambush, they began firing.

General Screven was wounded and taken prisoner by the English. Witnesses said that he was killed while a prisoner. Colonel Prevost's horse was shot, and the Americans thought that the English commander had been killed. Prevost, however, mounted another horse and advanced. Outnumbered, White retreated, destroying the bridges across the swamp until he reached Midway meetinghouse.

Here White wrote a letter to himself, purporting to be sent from Colonel Elbert. The fake letter ordered him to retreat, drawing the English toward Savannah, so that a large body of cavalry could attack from the rear. The letter was left so that Colonel Prevost found it. The ruse worked, and the English stopped their advance only six or seven miles beyond Midway meetinghouse.

Meanwhile, Daniel McGirth, reconnoitering toward Sunbury, learned that the forces under Colonel Fuser had not arrived. This also caused Colonel Prevost to abandon his pursuit of the Americans and return to St. Augustine. In his retreat Prevost burned Midway meetinghouse and all buildings in his path, and the region was ruthlessly plundered.

Colonel Fuser's fleet was delayed by headwinds, and he did not arrive at Sunbury until Prevost had retreated. Late in November, 1778, his ships, with five hundred men, battering cannon, light artillery, and mortars, sailed up Midway River toward Fort Morris, the only protection of Sunbury. Colonel John McIntosh, younger brother of George,

William, and Lachlan McIntosh, held Fort Morris with about one hundred Continental troops and militia and a few citizens from Sunbury. Colonel Fuser sent a letter threatening to burn Sunbury unless the fort was surrendered immediately.

John McIntosh did not hesitate. He sent back a letter stating that the Americans owned no property so valuable as the freedom for which they fought, and as for surrendering the fort, if Colonel Fuser wanted it, he would have to come and take it.

Colonel Fuser hesitated because he was waiting for a report from scouts he had sent out to discover where Colonel Prevost was. When the scouts reported that Prevost was on his way back to Florida, Fuser raised the siege and returned to the St. Johns River. When he met Prevost, each man blamed the other for the failure.

The Fall of Savannah

General Howe gathered his scattered forces together at Sunbury, all the while criticizing the way in which Colonel White had directed the skirmish at Midway. He also complained frequently to General Moultrie in South Carolina that he was not getting the support he needed or the supplies he had ordered, although he made no attempt to use the forces he had.

Meanwhile, Savannah was unprotected.

A deserter from the British ship *Neptune* was brought before Governor Houstoun on the sixth of December. His story left no doubt that Savannah was to be attacked by Colonel Campbell, who was coming from New York by sea. A message was sent to General Howe at Sunbury just as he received another message saying that General Augustine Prevost was marching against Georgia with all his forces from Florida. Leaving Major Joseph Lane in charge of Fort Morris, General Howe set out for Savannah with six hundred men.

Early in December the first of Colonel Campbell's ships arrived at

Tybee. By December 27 they had crossed the bar and were in the Savannah River.

General Howe called a council of war with his officers to decide whether he should retreat or defend the town. The majority voted to defend Savannah to the end.

On December 29, 1778, Howe placed Colonel Isaac Huger and his troops to guard the road that ran from Thunderbolt to Savannah. Although he was informed by Colonel George Walton that a private road ran through the swamp and that the enemy could use that road to by-pass the Americans and gain entrance to the town, General Howe ignored the warning and placed no troops on it.

When Colonel Campbell disembarked, he learned of the road from an old Negro named Quamino Dolly and at once paid him to be a guide. Using a gully to hide his movements, the British commanding officer, Sir James Baird, led the light infantry through the unguarded path which took them to the rear of the Americans. The English artillery, meanwhile, was stationed in a field in front of the American forces.

Sir James Baird attacked a small group of militia which was guarding the road to the Ogeechee Ferry. They were quickly put to flight. When these guns sounded, Colonel Campbell opened a heavy cannonade.

Attacked from the front and rear, the Americans panicked. A retreat was sounded, and they made their way helter-skelter toward Savannah.

The Georgia militia of about one hundred, under the command of Colonel Walton, received the worst of the attack by Sir James Baird. Walton was wounded, fell from his horse, and was captured. His forces met the enemy pursuing General Howe, and many were killed, wounded, or captured.

Colonel Elbert and his men fought until a retreat by the causeway was impossible. Reaching Musgrove Creek, Elbert found it filled by a high tide. Only those who could swim managed to cross; the others were either captured or drowned.

Sir Hyde Parker, the commander of the English fleet, moved his ships up to the town, preventing any communication between Savannah and South Carolina by water. He captured 126 prisoners, three ships, and eight smaller vessels; only one English seaman was killed and five wounded.

General Howe retreated to Cherokee Hill, about eight miles from Savannah, where he waited for the stragglers. He sent orders to Lieutenant Aaron Smith, who commanded the third South Carolina regiment at Ogeechee Ferry, and to Major Lane, whom he had left at Sunbury, to evacuate their posts and join him. Smith obeyed the order and arrived with twenty men, but Lane was persuaded by the citizens of Sunbury, who were afraid to be left unprotected, to remain behind. Later he was captured by General Prevost, and when he was exchanged and returned to the American army, he was court-martialed and dismissed for disobeying his general's order.

Howe crossed the Savannah River to South Carolina. Once again, Georgia was left to fight her enemies alone.

Ebenezer Betrayed

Colonel Campbell reached Cherokee Hill on the first of January, 1779, shortly after General Howe had left. As soon as he heard that Savannah had fallen, the Reverend Christopher Triebner, the minister at Ebenezer, who was a Loyalist, took the oath of allegiance to the king and accompanied the detachment of Campbell's troops that took his own village. Many of the Salzburgers did the same thing and received the guarantee of royal protection to their families and property.

Among those who remained Patriots were Governor Treutlen, William Holsendorf, and Joshua and Jacob Helfenstein. The Loyalists at Ebenezer harassed the Patriots in the settlement. They organized marauding parties of English and Loyalists and pillaged and burned every plantation or farm whose owner was suspected of being a Patriot.

The Salzburgers' church, which the English used first for a hospital and later for a stable. The bullet hole made by the soldiers in the weather vane can still be seen today.

Between Ebenezer and Savannah, Colonel Campbell fortified a string of forts. A company of British troops was stationed at Ebenezer, and the Salzburgers' brick church was used for a hospital. Later the English desecrated it by stabling their horses in it, and to show their contempt for the Salzburgers' religion they destroyed the church records. The soldiers used the metal weathervane atop the steeple, which was in the shape of a swan from Luther's coat of arms, as a target; the hole made by a musket ball can be seen today.

After Ebenezer was captured, prisoners from there and the surrounding countryside were taken to Savannah under a guard of ten soldiers. Sergeant William Jasper and a friend, Sergeant Newton, waited at a spring about two miles from Savannah. When the party of pris-

William Jasper and his friend Newton surprise the British at a spring near Ebenezer and free their prisoners.

oners arrived, the soldiers stacked their guns beside a tree to drink from the spring, leaving only two men to guard the prisoners. Sergeants Jasper and Newton sprang from their hiding place, shot the two guards, and took the English soldiers' muskets. With the aid of the released prisoners, they took the English soldiers to the American camp across the Savannah River. The spot is now named Jasper Springs. Jasper was killed at the siege of Savannah, and a county in Georgia was also named in his memory.

Having subdued the country around Savannah, Colonel Campbell planned to turn his attention toward Sunbury, but he learned that General Augustine Prevost had already taken that area. Sunbury's one thousand inhabitants watched the town being destroyed. The church was burned, and the crops laid waste. People from all over the state packed whatever they could carry, and in wagons, on horseback, or walking, they started toward South Carolina as refugees. Others turned Loyalist and joined the British forces.

General Howe also faced a court-martial for losing Savannah to the English. He was acquitted but was replaced by General Benjamin Lincoln, who arrived at Purrysburg early in January of 1779.

Augusta Captured

Only Augusta had not yet been taken, and in the middle of January Colonel Campbell set out with a thousand men to capture it. Although Generals Lincoln and Moultrie were camped just across the Savannah River at Purrysburg, their forces were not strong enough to stop the English.

General Elbert was sent by Lincoln to the upper part of South Carolina. He crossed the Savannah River and with a group of Georgia Patriots tried to prevent Colonel Campbell's crossing at Briar Creek. They failed and retreated slowly, skirmishing with Campbell's army as it approached Augusta. When Campbell reached the town, the American forces gave up Augusta without a struggle. Hundreds of Augustans collected their household goods and cattle and fled to South Carolina.

The Battle of Kettle Creek

American Colonels Andrew Pickens and John Dooly joined forces in the upper part of South Carolina, and after several unsuccessful skirmishes with the combined British and Loyalist forces under Colonel Boyd, a Loyalist leader, they crossed the river into Georgia and watched for an opportunity to attack. Unaware of the danger, Boyd stopped at a farm on the north side of Kettle Creek to rest. His men turned the horses loose to graze while they slaughtered cows and parched corn.

Pickens sent Captain Hugh McCall to scout Boyd's position. He reported that the enemy was unaware of the Americans.

As the Americans advanced, the pickets fired and retreated. Boyd hastily formed his line behind the shelter of a fence. He defended his position bravely but was driven back. While retreating, he was hit by three musket balls, two of which passed through his body. After an hour of fighting, the enemy crossed the creek and fled into the swamp, leaving their horses, baggage, and arms behind.

Pickens led the American forces through the swamp, and the battle began again on the other side of Kettle Creek. Finally, the enemy fled, leaving seventy of their men dead and seventy-five wounded or captured. Nine Americans were killed and twenty-three wounded.

Pickens ordered that Boyd receive all possible medical attention. The Loyalist leader thanked him for his civility and asked who had won the battle. When told that the Americans had won, the fatally wounded officer said that the outcome would have been different if he had not fallen.

He asked Colonel Pickens to bury him. He also gave him his personal articles and requested that Pickens send them to his wife with a letter telling her of his death and burial. The American carefully carried out the dying officer's wishes.

The Loyalists scattered. Some went to Florida, others joined the Creek and Cherokee Indians. A few returned to their homes and asked mercy from the Patriots, while some two hundred retreated to Augusta.

The prisoners captured at Kettle Creek were taken to South Carolina, tried for treason, and sentenced to death. Five were executed, the rest pardoned. The victory at Kettle Creek gave hope to the American cause, and several successful small incidents followed.

One of these took place when Colonel Elbert sent Lieutenant Benjamin Hawkins to find out how many were in the force holding Augusta. Hawkins wore an old British uniform as a disguise, and near an outpost at Bear Swamp he met three Loyalists. Since it was too late to avoid them, Lieutenant Hawkins advanced toward the men and asked

Robert Salette collects the reward for his own head.

who they were and where they were going. They said that they were on their way to join Colonel Daniel McGirth, the Loyalist leader.

Lieutenant Hawkins responded that he was McGirth and that he believed they were rebels and should be taken prisoner. The three men protested. Hawkins suggested that to demonstrate their friendship to the English they place their rifles on the ground and hold up their right hands. As soon as they did this, Lieutenant Hawkins took their rifles and ordered them to march ahead of him, threatening to shoot the first one who tried to escape. In this way he took them to the Americans' camp.

Another anecdote tells about Robert Sallette, an ardent Patriot who with a small band of men attacked the Loyalists at every chance. Finally, one prominent Loyalist offered £100 for the head of Robert Sallette, whom he had never seen. Hearing of the reward, Sallette disguised himself as a farmer, put a pumpkin in a bag, and rode to the home of the Loyalist. When the Loyalist asked if he had the head of Robert Sallette with him, Sallette replied that he did, but that he wanted to see the money before he delivered the head. The Loyalist counted out the £100, which Sallette put in his pocket. Then, pointing to his own head, he informed the Loyalist that it was the head of Robert Sallette. The Loyalist was so frightened that he ran from the room. Sallette left the pumpkin but took the money with him as he rode away.

CHAPTER ELEVEN

The Final Years

The American victory at Kettle Creek on February 14, 1779, alarmed the English enough for Colonel Campbell to give up Augusta and move southward. But the success of the Americans was short-lived.

In March, General Lincoln started to gather an army in the South, which would ultimately total eight thousand men. He planned to run the British forces out of the back country and then recover Savannah. The English numbered only four thousand men, and hopes were high for Lincoln's success.

The English, however, outmaneuvered the Americans. Colonel Mark Prevost surprised an army of two thousand under General John Ashe, camped where Briar Creek joins the Savannah River.

The English struck the American lines in the center, and they crumpled in five minutes, the men fleeing through the forest. Quickly Colonel Prevost turned on the right wing, and it too was scattered. The left wing under the command of Colonel Elbert fought furiously, and Prevost brought up his reserves. Nearly every American soldier was either killed, wounded, or captured in the bloody battle.

Elbert's stand was futile. The other Americans thrashed wildly through the swamps trying to escape. Those who could swim jumped into the river; some reached Carolina safely, but many were drowned.

When General Moultrie heard of the catastrophe, he said that it was nothing less than a total rout. In his opinion the defeat lengthened the war by a year, for if Ashe, who was on his way to join Lincoln, had arrived safely, the combined strength of their forces would have been enough to keep the British penned up at Savannah and a few other coastal towns, thus avoiding the disastrous campaign that followed.

Briar Creek had another unfortunate result. Many volunteers who were on their way to join General Lincoln turned around and went home, feeling that the Americans' cause was lost. Deep gloom settled on Georgia, but the leaders did not give up hope.

Governor Wright Returns

In Savannah, Colonel Campbell claimed that the entire province of Georgia was under English rule. He reinstated civil government in the colony to replace the military government that had been in effect since the fall of Savannah. He invited Georgians to return to their king and promised that Parliament would not tax the colonies.

In July, 1779, Governor Wright and Lieutenant Governor John Graham returned to Savannah from England and took up their duties.

Count Casimir Pulaski of Poland, who fought under George Washington and organized the American cavalry. He was shot in the attack on Savannah, and although the grape shot was removed by a French surgeon, he died a few days later and was buried at sea.

Count d'Estaing was an ambitious French admiral who saw a chance to add to his glory by helping the Americans take Savannah from the English. But his plan failed because he waited too long, thus giving the enemy an opportunity to fortify his position. In the bloody battle that followed he was wounded three times but lived—to be guillotined in Paris in 1794.

Wright did not find Georgia as well off as he had hoped. He did not think that there were enough English troops to protect it from the Americans who refused to accept the restored royal government. However, some of the Loyalists who had fled to Florida and the West Indies began slowly to return to the colony.

Now Georgia was expected to furnish food for the British armies in America. The supply officers claimed, however, that nothing but rice was available in Georgia and that the English troops and sailors did not like it.

The English also found the Indians unfriendly. They had thought that the Indians would flock to join their army, but they remained loyal to the Americans or neutral.

When Savannah fell to the king's troops, the Continental Congress and General Washington discussed the loss. They understood the importance of regaining the colony, but Washington said that he had no troops to spare. Henry Laurens from South Carolina kept the subject before Congress, and finally Congress requested that Virginia and North Carolina send what troops they could to General Lincoln in South Carolina. Congress also ordered Count Casimir Pulaski, a Polish nobleman who had offered his services to the Americans, and his legion of cavalry to the Southern Department.

Now, Lincoln had an idea. France had signed a treaty of alliance with the United States, and French Admiral Charles Henry Hector, Count d'Estaing, had brought a fleet to America to try to bottle up the Royal Navy in the Delaware River. The English had escaped, and Count d'Estaing agreed to come to Savannah and take part in what he saw as another chance to add to his triumphs.

Savannah in Danger

Savannah had been under English control for eight months when, before daybreak on Wednesday, September 8, 1779, Governor Wright received a note from General Prevost. The message confirmed the rumors of the past few days. Forty-two French ships of war had been sighted off Tybee.

The British were not prepared. Most of their army was at Beaufort, South Carolina, where it had stayed after failing to capture Charles Town a few months before. Another force was at Sunbury. Not more than a thousand military men were in Savannah. Beaufort was fifty miles from Savannah by water, and General Lincoln and his forces at Purrysburg commanded the land route.

General Lincoln called on every Patriot in South Carolina and Georgia for help. Down the river they marched: John Laurens with his regiment; Francis Marion, the Swamp Fox; Charles Cotesworth Pinckney; Thomas Heyward, Jr., a signer of the Declaration of Independence for South Carolina; General Isaac Huger, a Huguenot leader.

Count Pulaski with his cavalry advanced ahead of the American forces and crossed the Savannah River. General Lachlan McIntosh, who had been sent back to Georgia by General Washington, left Augusta with three companies of Georgia militia.

Troops from Virginia arrived without a single tent. The Continental troops had few supplies. Their arms consisted of rifles and old muskets. Dry moss was used for wadding. Shoes were mostly moccasins made from hides, and uniforms were hunting shirts of homespun or buckskin jackets. Only Pulaski's troops were well equipped and mounted.

The English in Savannah had hardly twelve hundred troops to man a line over twelve hundred feet long on the river bluff. General Prevost sent a hurried appeal to St. Augustine and a message to Lieutenant Colonel John Maitland, the commanding officer in Beaufort, telling him to come at once. By the twelfth, both the land and sea routes were blocked, but Maitland left Beaufort with eight hundred troops in a small fleet of boats.

About the same time, Count d'Estaing began landing his men at a bluff overlooking the Vernon River. Many of the men had been in open boats for three nights, and when they met no opposition, they soon had a big copper kettle filled with soup heating over a fire.

The next day d'Estaing sent a greeting to Count Pulaski at the Habersham plantation on the Ogeechee Road. The Polish hero had come to help the Americans because of his love of freedom, but he had found them lacking in continental culture, and he was delighted that the French had arrived.

D'Estaing led two thousand French toward Savannah on the fourteenth of September, and on the night of the fifteenth they camped four miles from the town. Along the way the French confiscated thirteen steers, ten cows, five sheep, thirty-nine hogs, fifty fowl, and twenty gallons of Jamaica rum.

The English Gain Time

The next morning Count d'Estaing, under a truce, demanded immediate surrender. General Prevost stalled. He said that he must confer with Governor Wright. Prevost hoped that, if he could hold out long enough, Colonel Maitland would somehow get to Savannah. The king's officer suggested a twenty-four-hour truce to consider the question of surrender. Count d'Estaing agreed. The English had gained a day in which to strengthen their fortifications.

Since the English had first seen the French fleet off Tybee the week before, they had labored day and night on their defensive works. Five hundred slaves were put to work building nine new redoubts. Houses near the town which might provide cover for the enemy were burned. Cannon were brought from naval vessels, and seamen were assigned to batteries.

Civilians and the clergy pitched in. The Reverend John Zubly became chaplain, and his church was turned into a hospital.

Meanwhile, Maitland and his men moved south through the inland waterways of Carolina. A Charles Town newspaper reported that the English garrison had embarked, but apparently d'Estaing and Lincoln received no information of the enemy movements.

As Maitland approached the Savannah River, he could see the French ships barring the channel. Some Negro fishermen told him that there was a waterway behind Dawfuskie Island where a shallow cut joined two creeks. The passage was usable only at high tide, but it would put them into the Savannah River above the French ships. Maitland decided to try it. The cut was so shallow that the men had to get out of the boats and, struggling through the mud up to their waists, drag the vessels behind them. When they reached the river, all they could see were alligators lying in the mud. No French ship was that far up the river.

On September 16, shortly after d'Estaing had sent his demand to Prevost, Maitland and the first of his men arrived in Savannah. Admiral d'Estaing learned that the English reinforcements had arrived after he had granted Prevost's request for a twenty-four-hour delay. On the morning of the seventeenth, General Lincoln and Count d'Estaing watched fourteen boats carrying twenty-five men each sail up the Savannah River and disembark.

The arrival of Colonel Maitland's troops cheered the English. Maitland himself was sick with a fever, but he strode into Governor Wright's council room and announced that any man who recommended surrender would be his enemy.

D'Estaing Decides on a Siege

When the twenty-four-hour truce had passed, d'Estaing still did not attack. He offered excuses, saying that all of his troops were not ashore, that General McIntosh had not sent down flatboats from Augusta, and that Lincoln's troops had not crossed the Savannah River on time. Since Colonel Maitland had arrived with reinforcements, there was little chance of taking Savannah by assault. The only thing to do was to lay siege to it.

The Americans were optimistic, even though the leaders knew that d'Estaing had made a serious mistake by waiting until the English were better prepared. But the French forces were discontented. The regulars did not want to fight with the American militiamen, finding their dress and manners uncouth, nor would they associate with the several hundred free Negro troops which d'Estaing had brought from Santo Domingo and whom he insisted should be treated like regulars. Even d'Estaing's officers grumbled. Many of them thought that the French commander was using them to achieve his own glory.

Three weeks had passed since the French fleet arrived, but the American and French allies had only dug a few trenches and brought ashore some cannon and mortars from the French ships.

On the night of October 3, the allies began to bombard Savannah. In the next five days nearly every building in town was damaged, and as many as fifty shells hit some of the houses.

As the bombardment continued day after day, the citizens grew accustomed to it. The Negro children soon discovered a profitable pastime. When a hot cannonball fell, they would run out into the street and cover it with sand. After the ball had cooled, they took it to an English officer, who paid them sixpence each for the ammunition, which the English used to fire back at the Americans.

As the English batteries returned the allies' fire, the Americans continued to fortify their position. Officers and men worked together. One day, as Major Thomas Pinckney was helping dig a trench, a shell burst very close by. It covered him with sand, but he brushed himself off and went on with his work.

The French troops grew more and more discontented. The supply of bread had run out, and the French soldiers did not like rice. They had eaten all of the pigs, turkeys, and beef they could find in the countryside, and things were even worse on board the ships, where nothing was left but two-year-old bread. A navy officer wrote in his journal that scurvy was so bad on the ships that about thirty-five men died each day and were thrown into the sea. Many of the French officers wanted to sail away and leave the siege, but d'Estaing decided to attack.

The English Withstand Attack

General Lincoln agreed to d'Estaing's plan, since he had no alternative. General Pulaski also proposed a plan of assault. He suggested that the French attack along the Augusta road, the Americans under General McIntosh attack the left wing, and he and his cavalry would attack the center of the English line. D'Estaing insisted that the French must lead every assault, followed by the Americans and Pulaski. October ninth was the date set for the attack.

Everything went wrong for the allies. The French were late arriving at the American camp, and d'Estaing blamed it on the American guides. French military etiquette required that certain regiments precede others, and even within regiments companies were given preference by the date of commission of their captains.

By five o'clock in the morning only the front lines had reached the edge of the woods, and as daylight broke, the troops grew restless. The English sentinels had discovered their presence, and the element of surprise was lost.

D'Estaing did not wait for the troops to complete their formation but ordered the drummers to beat the charge. The vanguard attacked, but they were not reinforced and the English drove them back. Count d'Estaing was wounded in the arm, but he continued to direct the assault. Three times he rallied the French troops and tried to send them through the English lines. Despite the officers' threats, however, they could not move forward in the face of the heavy fire.

Baron Curt Von Stedingk, a Swedish officer, managed to reach the entrenchments north of Spring Hill redoubt and personally planted the American flag there. The Americans under Lachlan McIntosh came up behind Stedingk's troops, but the slaughter was so great that they were forced to retreat. Arriving with General McIntosh's column, Major Thomas Pinckney and Colonel John Laurens were cut off from their command.

The grape shot (actual size) that mortally wounded Count Pulaski.

Count Pulaski with his cavalry waited at the edge of the woods. He was to enter Savannah when a breach had been made by the infantry. When he saw what was happening at the front and heard that d'Estaing was wounded, he charged. He was hit by grapeshot and died a few days later.

During the last minutes of fighting, d'Estaing was hit again. This time he fell and was found by one of his officers lying among the dead but still alive.

Only one hour after the attack began, the retreat was sounded. The American officers tried to gather their troops, but many of the men had been lost in the swamps. As soon as the retreat began, Colonel Maitland ordered a counterattack, but the French troops stationed near the old Jewish burial ground held their ground, and the English returned to Savannah to celebrate their victory.

Before d'Estaing had arrived at Savannah, the British commander in chief, Sir Henry Clinton, had assembled a fleet in New York with which he planned to capture Charles Town. Clinton waited to find out what had happened at Savannah, and as soon as he learned of the English victory, the Charles Town expedition moved forward. It sailed late in December, 1779, and arrived at the mouth of the Savannah River at the end of January, 1780. The English made their base and set up depots on Tybee Island.

Clinton called in all the English and Loyalist troops in Georgia to help him take Charles Town. General Lincoln took all the Continental troops from Georgia to defend Charles Town, despite the protests of the Georgia Patriots.

Lincoln surrendered to General Clinton on May 12, 1780, and he and his entire army became prisoners of war. The fall of Charles Town has been called the worst military defeat in America's history, up to Bataan in World War Two. Clinton then returned to New York but left General Charles Lord Cornwallis with a force of English troops to occupy the Carolinas and Georgia.

The Mackay House

One of the most infamous Loyalists of the entire war was a man named Thomas Brown. When the first liberty pole was erected in Savannah on June 5, 1775, Brown, who lived in Augusta, was loyally celebrating the king's birthday. He openly scoffed at the proceedings of the Continental Congress, and a group of Patriots seized him, tarred and feathered him, and rode him through the streets in a cart drawn by three mules. Brown never forgave them this indignity.

Brown joined the Florida Rangers and was made a colonel. He was ruthless toward the Patriot side; neither man, woman, nor child received mercy from him.

After Savannah had fallen to the English and Archibald Campbell had taken Augusta in January, 1779, he left Brown in command there. Brown took his revenge. He promptly ordered all Patriots banished from the city and their property confiscated. He sent groups of Loyalists into the countryside to search out Patriot leaders, and Colonel John Dooly was murdered before the eyes of his wife and children.

Elijah Clarke and Hugh McCall began to gather forces to take

When the Americans tried to take Augusta from the Loyalists and English, Colonel Thomas Brown, infamous Loyalist leader, took refuge in the Mackay House, which was a trading post. For five days the Americans laid siege, but when they learned that reinforcements were coming, they gave up and retreated.

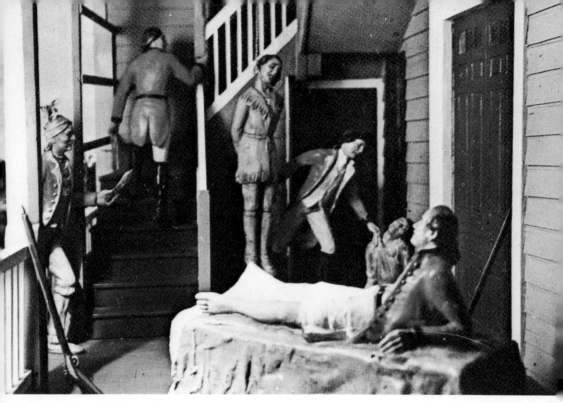

When the Patriots retreated from the Mackay House, they had to leave behind Captain Ashley and twenty-eight wounded men. Although Colonel Brown was wounded also, he ordered that the prisoners be hanged and lay on his cot enjoying their last death struggles.

Augusta from Brown. With about two hundred men they approached the city. Colonel McCall was to enter by the lower road; Major Samuel Taylor approached by the upper road, and Colonel Clarke went by the center road. Taylor came upon an Indian camp, which he attacked, and the retreating Indians gave Brown the first warning of the approaching enemy.

The Indians made their way to Mackay's trading post, a large house that had been taken over by Brown. Fortifying themselves here, the Loyalists resisted a five-day siege. Brown managed to send a messenger to the fort at Ninety-Six, South Carolina, asking for help. When Clarke learned that five hundred reinforcements were on the way to Augusta, he raised the siege.

When the Americans retreated, they were forced to leave behind twenty-nine men who were so badly wounded that they could not travel. They were taken prisoner, and thirteen of them were hanged from the outside stairs of the Mackay house, while Brown lay wounded on a cot, enjoying their final struggles.

Nancy Hart Does Her Share

Throughout 1780 and 1781, fighting went on in the South between General Cornwallis and the Americans under Generals Horatio Gates and Nathanael Greene in the Carolinas. So far as the military commanders on both sides were concerned, Georgia was finished. Georgia soldiers fought in South Carolina at such conflicts as Ninety-Six and Cowpens, and General Greene commended them for their bravery.

In the back country of Georgia, Patriots continued to harass the Loyalists at every opportunity, and Nancy Hart was one of these. Nancy had come to Georgia from North Carolina. She married Captain

Major General Nathanael Greene.

Nancy Hart capturing the Loyalists.

Benjamin Hart, an ancestor of Thomas Hart Benton, the famous artist.

Nancy lived in the Georgia back country with her husband and children. She was a good cook, and it was said that she could prepare pumpkin seven different ways—one for each day of the week. Nancy was a big, good-natured woman with red hair, and she was cross-eyed.

One morning, not long after John Dooly, the Patriot leader, had been murdered at his home nearby, five of the murderers appeared at the Harts' cabin. Only Nancy and the children were in the house, Captain Hart having gone to meet some friends in the woods nearby.

The Loyalists demanded breakfast, and Nancy agreeably set out pumpkin pie, venison, a hoecake, and fresh honeycomb. To show that she was friendly, Nancy took a swallow from the jug of corn liquor that one of the Loyalists offered her.

Her hospitality fooled the men, and they stacked their guns in a corner and sat down to enjoy breakfast. When they were seated, Nancy stepped quietly to the wall and snatched down an old fowling piece. Pointing it at her guests, she told them that she would blow out the brains of the first man who made a move to get up or taste her food. Behind her stood her oldest daughter, Sukey, ready with another loaded gun to hand her mother if she needed it. Meanwhile, Nancy had sent one of the children to find Captain Hart.

The Loyalists were embarrassed at having been taken so easily by a woman, but as each soldier looked at Nancy's crossed eyes, he thought that she was aiming her gun directly at him.

At last, one of the men, thinking she was not serious, stood up from his chair, but the minute he moved, Nancy fired, and he dropped dead. Before another could move, she had exchanged muskets with Sukey and was ready again.

Just then, her husband returned with a group of Patriots, and in less than half an hour all of the Loyalists were hanged.

A Black Man Substitutes for a White Man

Austin Dabney was another outstanding figure in the Revolution. When the back country of Georgia began to be settled, a Mr. Aycock migrated there from North Carolina. He brought with him a young mulatto boy named Austin Dabney.

When the war started, Mr. Aycock sent Austin into the army as his substitute, and the eighteen-year-old boy proved to be a good soldier. He fought in many of the skirmishes in the back country and served under Elijah Clarke at the Battle of Kettle Creek.

Austin was wounded in the thigh, and a man named Harris took him home and nursed him. Austin felt that he owed his life to Mr. Harris, and he stayed with the white family after the war was over. He drew a pension from the United States Government because of his broken thigh, and the legislature of Georgia gave him a tract of land in Walton County.

Savannah Evacuated

The defeat of Cornwallis at Yorktown did not end the war in Georgia. The English still held Savannah and had no intention of giving it up until they were forced to do so.

General Washington sent General Nathanael Greene to the South to clear the British out of Charles Town and Savannah. To help Greene, Washington sent General Anthony Wayne. In South Carolina, Wayne asked Greene to let him have some of his old Pennsylvania troops for the Georgia campaign, but Greene needed the experienced soldiers for the attack on Charles Town. He gave General Wayne five hundred men, and they crossed the Savannah River into Georgia.

The state government was disorganized, and the Georgia militia could supply Wayne with only five hundred raw infantry. Food and supplies were nonexistent, so Wayne sent to South Carolina for rice and beef for his soldiers and divided it with the half-starved civilians. To get additional recruits he sent messengers secretly into Savannah and offered two hundred acres of land, a cow, and two hogs to any English or Loyalist troops who would desert and join the Americans, but he got less than a hundred men by that means.

General Greene had ordered Wayne to stay at Bethesda until he received orders to attack Savannah. Wayne became bored and took to drinking and, because of the inactivity, he relaxed his vigilance. No one noticed the Indian spies around the camp. They were from a group of Creeks who were on their way to Savannah to join the English. The Indians had learned that the camp was poorly guarded, and one night when the Americans had only one sentry and a few guards on duty, the Indians attacked.

They killed the sentry and with wild war whoops swarmed toward the camp, but the main camp was farther than they had estimated, and their cries aroused the Americans in time.

General Wayne was one of the first out of his tent with pistol in one

158

hand and sword in the other. He rallied the command from its confusion, and the attack was repelled. This surprise attack, on the night of June 23, 1782, was the last battle of the Revolution for General Wayne.

In Savannah, Governor Wright received word that Parliament was planning to give up all the American colonies. Although Wright felt that England should have kept Savannah unless it was recaptured, he carried out his orders and proposed to General Wayne that hostilities cease. Wayne refused and referred the matter to General Greene in South Carolina, who in turn laid the offer before the Continental Congress.

The decision was finally made when Governor Wright received word from Sir Guy Carleton to evacuate immediately both Savannah and the province of Georgia.

General Wayne invited Colonel James Jackson, a Georgian who had fought valiantly for the American cause all during the war, to assume the honor of receiving the keys to the city of Savannah. On July 12, 1782, three and a half years after the capital of Georgia fell to the English, the Americans marched down the streets of Savannah again.

CHAPTER TWELVE

Freedom Brings Responsibilities

W hen the Americans got the freedom they had demanded from the established government of England, they found it necessary to take on the responsibilities of self-government. It seemed easy enough to elect a governor and assembly, but it was another matter to carry out all the functions necessary to make the government effective.

A Government of Confusion

John Adam Treutlen had been elected the first governor of the new State of Georgia in 1777. Savannah was the capital, and Treutlen managed to keep things in good order. When the General Assembly of South Carolina voted to annex Georgia and make one state of the two, Governor Treutlen was the chief opponent and prevented the annexation.

In 1778, John Houstoun was elected governor, but in December of that year Savannah fell to the English, and the seat of government was moved first to Ebenezer and then to Augusta. In January of the following year, however, Colonel Archibald Campbell took Augusta. The Colonial Records were sent to South Carolina for safekeeping, and even though the elected heads of the state tried to carry on some semblance of organized meetings, their efforts failed.

In July, 1779, only twenty-five members of the council met in Augusta. Recognizing the impossibility of holding a popular election, they appointed a Supreme Executive Council, composed of nine men whom they empowered to run the state government in any way they might be able. There was little for them to do. The treasury was empty. Paper bills of credit issued by the state were worthless. It was useless to try to levy taxes, because no one had any money.

To add to the confusion, in November of 1779 another group of Georgians met and elected a new Executive Council, with George Walton as governor. In January, 1780, Richard Howlet took Walton's place. For a short time there were two governing bodies claiming supremacy in Georgia.

As the English began to lose ground in the colonies and Augusta once more became the property of the Georgians, the council met there again, and Dr. Nathan Brownson was elected governor in August of 1781. In January, 1782, John Martin succeeded him, and Martin had the good fortune to be in office when Governor Wright was evacuated from Savannah.

The Colonial Records of Georgia traveled extensively during the Revolution. After the fall of Savannah, they were sent to Charles Town. When the English threatened to attack that city, the Georgia records were carried in wagons by Captain John Milton to New Bern, North Carolina. As the enemy moved into North Carolina, the records were removed to Maryland, where they stayed until the end of the war, when they were gathered up and returned to Savannah.

Georgia—One of the United States

The war had taken a heavy toll of the city of Savannah. Damage from the siege had not been repaired, and churches and public buildings still showed signs of their wartime use as hospitals. The people of Georgia did not stop to mourn or question whether the war was worth the price. They started the long job of constructing their state.

More and more settlers migrated to the back country from the northern states, and Augusta grew rapidly. Savannah remained the capital of the state, and gradually private homes and public buildings were repaired or rebuilt. Estates formerly owned by Loyalists were auctioned or given to soldiers and officers as payment for their services.

The assembly, now called the State Legislature, met in January, 1783, and Dr. Lyman Hall was elected governor. George Walton was chief justice; Samuel Stirk, attorney general; John Martin, treasurer; John Milton, secretary of state; and Richard Call, surveyor general.

Lachlan McIntosh, John Houstoun, and Edward Telfair were appointed to settle and adjust the northern boundaries of Georgia with South Carolina. When the boundaries of all the states in the new nation were finally established, Georgia was found to be the largest state east of the Mississippi River, and it remains so today.

When the legislature met again in July, 1783, Governor Lyman Hall presented the first complete picture of the state and its resources. He pointed out that military defenses must be established, that land laws must be revised, schools must be built, and debts must be paid. All of

When Georgia announced its independence in 1776 and became a state, a convention was called to formulate a constitution. A new seal was adopted, which was said to be the design of Button Gwinnett.

these things would require money, and therefore, the people of Georgia must be taxed.

This time, however, taxation would not be without representation. They would be represented by officials of their own choosing in their State Legislature.

More important, Georgia was no longer alone in her struggle for survival. She had become a part of the United States of America.

Bibliography

READING LIST

Bailey, Bernadine, *Picture Book of Georgia*. Chicago: Albert Whitman & Co., 1966.

Blackburn, Joyce, *James Edward Oglethorpe*. Philadelphia: J. B. Lippincott, 1970.

Cate, Margaret David, *Early Days of Coastal Georgia*. St. Simons Island, Ga.: Fort Frederica Association, 1955.

Coleman, Kenneth, *Georgia History in Outline*. Athens, Ga.: University of Georgia Press, 1960.

Evans, Lawton B., *All About Georgia*. New York: American Book Company, 1933.

Godley, Margaret, and Bragg, Lillian, *Stories of Old Savannah*. Savannah, Ga.: Privately printed, 1949.

FURTHER READING

Anderson, Mary, and others, *Georgia: A Pageant of Years*. Richmond: Garrett and Massie, 1933.

Broucek, Jack W., *Eighteenth-Century Music in Savannah, Georgia*. Unpublished thesis, Tallahassee, Fla.: Florida State *University*, 1963.

Church, Leslie F., *Oglethorpe: A Study of Philanthropy in England and Georgia*. London: Epworth Press, 1932.

Coleman, Kenneth, *The American Revolution in Georgia, 1763–1789*. Athens, Ga.: University of Georgia Press, 1958.

Coulton, E. Merton, ed., *Georgia's Disputed Ruins*. Chapel Hill, N.C.: University of North Carolina Press, 1937.

——— *A Short History of Georgia*. Chapel Hill, N.C.: University of North Carolina Press, 1933.

Georgia Historical Quarterly, Vol. XX, No. 4 (December, 1936), and Vol. XXIII, No. 4 (December, 1939).

Jones, Charles C., *History of Georgia*, Vols. 1 and 2. Boston: Houghton Mifflin Company, 1883.

Knight, Lucian Lamar, *A Standard History of Georgia and Georgians*. Chicago: Lewis Publishing Company, 1917.

Lamb, Harold, *New Found World*. Garden City, N.Y.: Doubleday and Company, 1955.

Lanning, John Tate, *The Spanish Missions of Georgia*. Chapel Hill, N.C.: University of North Carolina Press, 1935.

Lawrence, Alexander A., *Storm over Savannah*. Athens, Ga.: University of Georgia Press, 1951.

Lovell, Caroline Couper, *The Golden Isles of Georgia*. Boston: Little, Brown and Company, 1939.

Lowery, Woodbury, *The Spanish Settlements Within the Present Limits of the United States and Florida*, Vols. 1 and 2. New York: G.P. Putnam's Sons, 1911.

McCullar, Bernice, *This Is Your Georgia*. Northport, Ala.: American Southern Publishing Company, 1966.

Norman, Charles, *Discoverers of America*. New York: Thomas Y. Crowell, 1968.

Reese, Trevor Richard, *Colonial Georgia*. Athens, Ga.: University of Georgia Press, 1963.

Smith, Paul R., *Loyalists and Redcoats*. Chapel Hill, N.C.: University of North Carolina Press, 1964.

Stephens, William, *The Colonial Records of the State of Georgia*, Vol. 4 and Supplement. Atlanta: Franklin-Turner, 1908.

Stokes, Thomas L., *The Savannah*. Rivers of America Series. New York: Rinehart and Company, 1951.

Swanton, John R., *Early History of the Creek Indians and Their Neighbors*. Washington, D.C.: United States Government Printing Office, 1922.

———— *The Indians of the Southeastern United States*. Smithsonian Institution Bureau of American Ethnology, Bulletin 137. Washington, D.C.: United States Government Printing Office, 1946.

Tailfer, Patrick, and others, *A True and Historical Narrative of the Colony of Georgia; With Comments by the Earl of Egmont*. Athens, Ga.: University of Georgia Press, 1960.

Writers' Program, Works Progress Administration *Georgia: A Guide to Its Towns and Countryside*. Athens, Ga.: University of Georgia Press, 1940.

Important Dates

8000 B.C. to
A.D. 1717   Indians, the prehistoric settlers of Georgia roamed over the state, leaving their history in mounds and artifacts.

1539   Hernando de Soto landed with an army of Spanish noblemen and soldiers on the coast of what is now Florida and began his march through Georgia searching for gold.

1564   Admiral Pedro Menéndez slaughtered the French Huguenots at Fort Caroline and founded St. Augustine.

1670   The English founded a colony at Charles Town, South Carolina, and began to squeeze the Spaniards out of Guale.

1733   February 12, James Edward Oglethorpe and the first colonists landed on Yamacraw Bluff and began the settlement of Savannah, Georgia.

1736   In February, Oglethorpe and a group of new settlers he had brought from England began work on the town and fort of Frederica.

1742   On July 4, the Spaniards appeared off St. Simons Island to attack Oglethorpe and the English at Fort Frederica. The English defeated the Spaniards at the Battle of Bloody Marsh, and the Spaniards never again attacked the English colonies.

1743   Oglethorpe returned to England, leaving Georgia to govern itself.

1752   The trustees gave up their charter to Georgia and the colony became a royal province.

1776   On August 10, the Declaration of Independence was read in Savannah.

1778   General Robert Howe lost Savannah to the English.

1779   The Patriots were unable to recapture Savannah even with the help of French allies.

1781   When Cornwallis surrendered at Yorktown on October 19, Savannah was still held by the English.

1782   Governor James Wright received direct orders from Sir Guy Carleton to evacuate both Savannah and Georgia. On July 12, the Americans took possession of the city.

Historic Sites

MACON

Ocmulgee National Monument. In the museum at Ocmulgee, artifacts and dioramas trace the six successive occupations by different Indian groups from about 8000 B.C. to A.D. 1717. Outside, a restored earth lodge is open to the visitor.

CARTERSVILLE

Etowah Mounds Archaeological Area. This excavation of an Indian ceremonial center is west of US 411 and US 41 near Cartersville.

EATONTON

Eagle Effigy Mound. Made of white quartz boulders, this rock mound is in the shape of a spread eagle, 102 feet long and 120 feet wide.

SAVANNAH

Oglethorpe's Bench. This marble bench, located just west of City Hall on Yamacraw Bluff, is a memorial to the site on which Oglethorpe pitched his tent in which he lived for nearly a year while Savannah was being built.

The Trustees' Garden. When Savannah was laid out by Oglethorpe, this garden was part of the overall plan. Its purpose was to furnish vegetables, shrubs, and trees for the settlers, especially mulberry trees for feeding silkworms.

The Herb House. Built in 1734 to house the tools of the gardeners of the Trustees' Garden, this is said to be the oldest standing building in Georgia.

The Pirates' House. This building at 20 East Broad Street is said to have been built in 1754 for a seamen's tavern. It is now a part of the Pirates' House Restaurant.

426 East St. Julian Street. This house, built between 1750 and 1790, is in the design of modest colonial homes. The windows have six panes over nine.

Johnson Square. The first square laid off by Oglethorpe and named for Governor Robert Johnson of South Carolina, who helped the early settlers to build their town of Savannah. Here the sundial was placed and a public well dug. Facing the square was the general store, the house for strangers, public oven, and gristmill. A mosaic map near the sundial shows the early city in colorful tiles.

Wright Square. This square was laid out in 1733 but was later named Wright Square for Governor James Wright, last of the royal governors of Georgia. In the southeast corner is a massive granite boulder, carved from Stone Mountain, which commemorates the burial of Tomochichi in 1739.

Independent Presbyterian Church. The congregation of this church was organized in 1755. John Zubly, the minister who changed his mind, was serving here at the time of the Revolution. The original building burned, and the present church is of later architecture.

Statue of James Edward Oglethorpe. In the center of Chippewa Square is a magnificent bronze figure of James Edward Oglethorpe which was designed by Daniel Chester French. The figure faces south toward Oglethorpe's enemy, the Spanish, whom he defeated in 1742 at the Battle of Bloody Marsh.

De Soto Hilton Hotel. Built on the spot where Hernando De Soto is said to have rested his troops en route to the Mississippi River. During the Revolutionary War, military barracks were erected here.

Madison Square. This square features a monument to Sergeant William Jasper, who made himself a hero by replacing the flag on the battlements of Fort Moultrie during the siege of Charleston. Jasper fought bravely at the siege of Savannah in 1779 and was killed there.

Monterey Square. The monument here is to Count Casimir Pulaski, the Polish nobleman who was killed at the siege of Savannah.

Temple Mickve Israel. On the east side of Monterey Square stands the present-day temple of Georgia's oldest Jewish congregation. The group of Spanish-Portuguese Jews who landed in Savannah just five months after the founding of the colony, brought with them a Sephar Torah, which is still a prized possession of the congregation today.

Hodgson Hall. Headquarters of the Georgia Historical Society, oldest such society in Georgia. It contains the full-length portrait of the Right Honorable Selina, Countess of Huntingdon, to whom George Whitefield left Bethesda at his death.

Wesley Monumental Methodist Church. On the corner of Abercorn and Gordon streets stands a Gothic Revival building which is a memorial to John Wesley and Charles Wesley. The stained-glass windows were made by Tiffany and the Wesley Window contains the busts of the two men.

Colonial Park Cemetery. This burial ground was opened about 1750 and was closed to burials one hundred years later. Among those buried here were Archibald Bulloch, James Habersham, and Hugh McCall, Georgia's first historian.

Eppinger Tavern. At 110 East Oglethorpe Avenue stands what is believed to be the oldest brick house in Georgia. It was built about 1770 for use as a tavern by John Eppinger.

Greene Square. Named for General Nathanael Greene, who fought in Georgia during the Revolution and died near Savannah.

Lutheran Church of the Ascension. On the east side of Wright Square now stands the Lutheran Church of the Ascension. It was organized in 1741 by the Salzburger pastor, John Martin Bolzius of Ebenezer.

Christ Episcopal Church. On the east side of Johnson Square stands Christ Episcopal Church on the same lot where the first Church of England parish was built when Savannah was founded. John Wesley and George Whitefield preached here.

Wormsloe Plantation. The home of Noble Jones, one of Georgia's first colonists, Wormsloe is the only Savannah plantation still in the possession of its original owners. The remains of a tabby fort built in 1741 can still be seen. The plantation is often open to the public in the spring.

Bethesda. The oldest existing orphanage in America, founded by the Reverend George Whitefield in 1740, today provides a home for boys with educational, vocational, and cultural programs.

Beaulieu. First settled as the plantation home of William Stephens, this small community on the Vernon River is the site at which Count d'Estaing landed his forces in 1779 to help the Patriots try to recover Savannah from the English.

Vernonburg. The town of Vernonburg was settled in 1742 by German-Swiss immigrants who made silk. It is now Chatham County's smallest town.

MIDWAY

Midway Museum is a memorial to the ardent Patriots at Midway when the Revolution started.

Fort Morris. Revolutionary fort where Colonel John McIntosh made the famous statement: "Come and take it." The fort is ten miles east of US 17 at Midway.

DARIEN

Fort King George. First this was the site of a Spanish mission while Spain was attempting to colonize Guale. In 1721 Colonel John Barnwell of South Carolina built Fort King George here. Remains of the fort are on the Altamaha River and can be seen east of US 17 at Darien.

ST. SIMONS ISLAND

Fort Frederica. The site of the town built by Oglethorpe for the defense of Georgia and the colonies is now a national monument. Foundations of the houses and fort have been excavated and are open to the public.

Battle of Bloody Marsh. A monument marks the spot where English soldiers ambushed the Spaniards who were headed for Frederica and completely routed them.

EBENEZER

The original brick church built by the Salzburgers before the Revolutionary War still stands on the bank of the Savannah River about fifteen miles north of Savannah. A hole shot by an English soldier can be seen in the weathervane.

AUGUSTA

The Mackay House. John Francis Williams and his trading partner, Robert Mackay, built this house in which Mackay, his wife, and son lived and where they conducted a trading post until his death in 1775. In 1780 Colonel Elijah Clark, a Patriot leader, attempted to take the Mackay House, then held by a company of English soldiers and Cherokee Indians. The Patriots were unsuccessful, and twenty-nine wounded Patriots were captured and hanged in the stairwell of the house.

Meadow Garden. After the Revolutionary War, George Walton, one of the signers of the Declaration of Independence and governor of Georgia, made his home at Meadow Garden on a two-hundred-acre tract of land on the edge of Augusta. He died here on February 2, 1804. His body now lies at the Signers' Monument in front of the courthouse in Augusta.

Signers' Monument. The bodies of George Walton and Lyman Hall, signers of the Declaration of Independence, are buried in crypts beneath a shaft erected in honor of the signers. The location of Button Gwinnett's grave has never been determined for certain.

170

Index

About the Author

Clifford Sheats Capps is a native of Carrollton, Georgia, who now makes her home in Atlanta. For many years she taught school in Fulton County, Georgia, and she has always been interested in the history of her home state, especially since her family has long been prominent in Georgia life. At age thirteen Mrs. Capps won first place and a five-dollar gold piece in a nationwide story-writing contest, and since then she has published various articles and stories. COLONIAL GEORGIA is her first full-length book.

Eugenia Burney's great-great-great-great-great-grandfather, Jacob Griner, was a Salzburger who came to Georgia in 1734 and settled at Ebenezer. Although Miss Burney was born in South Carolina, she spent many summer vacations on the Griner plantation in Bulloch County. COLONIAL GEORGIA is the author's second book for Nelson. She and her husband, Gardell Dano Christensen, now live on the Griner plantation, which is located in Brooklet, near Savannah, and has been in the Griner family for more than a century.

Colonial Histories

The thirteen colonies that formed the nucleus of a new nation in 1776 have a history stretching back to the first settlements almost as long as their record as states of the union. Americans have always been aware of their heritage, but because of the bicentennial celebration there is a growing interest in the period leading up to the Declaration of Independence. This series of histories on each of the original colonies brings to life the men and events of that formative era.

Letters, eyewitness reports, maps, prints, and documents highlight the text. By limiting the scope of the series it has been possible to include the colorful details that make the colonial period vivid. A determined effort has been made to "tell it like it was" on subjects such as treatment of the Indians and indentured servants, slavery, and the hardships many colonists endured. Information on historic sites and restorations is a useful guide for tourists. This series is recommended for students, teachers, and the general reader with an interest in America's colonial past.